PRACTICAL
GRACE

Other Books by Robert K. Hudnut

Call Waiting: How to Hear God Speak

Emerson's Aesthetic

Meeting God in the Darkness

This People, This Parish

The Bootstrap Fallacy:
What the Self-Help Books Don't Tell You

Church Growth Is Not the Point

Arousing the Sleeping Giant:
How to Organize Your Church for Action

The Sleeping Giant:
Arousing Church Power in America

A Thinking Man and the Christ

A Sensitive Man and the Christ

An Active Man and the Christ

Surprised by God: What It Means to Be a Minister
in Middle-Class America Today

PRACTICAL

How to Find God in the Everyday

GRACE

ROBERT K. HUDNUT

Abingdon Press
NASHVILLE

PRACTICAL GRACE
How to Find God in the Everyday

Library of Congress Cataloging-in-Publication Data

Hudnut, Robert K.
    Practical grace : how to find God in the everyday / Robert K. Hudnut.
        pages cm
    ISBN 978-1-4267-5326-8 (pbk. : alk. paper)   1. Christian life—Prayers and devotions.   2. Grace (Theology)—Prayers and devotions.   I. Title.
    BV4501.3.H821825 2013
    242'.2—dc23

                                                                            2013008029

13 14 15 16 17 18 19 20 21 22—10 9 8 7 6 5 4 3 2 1

MANUFACTURED IN THE UNITED STATES OF AMERICA

For Bud Philbrook, exemplar of grace

The glory of God is a person fully alive.
—Irenaeus, second-century bishop

By grace you have been saved through faith; and
this is not your own doing, it is the gift of God.
—Ephesians 2:8

CONTENTS

Contents

Contents

Contents

Contents

Contents

PREFACE

It's all grace. Everything is grace. Everything. The good, the bad, the best, the worst—everything. "By grace you have been saved," the Bible says (Eph. 2:8). Grace is God in action.

When we lose our job, it's grace. When we get a bad grade, it's grace. When we fall ill, it's grace. God doesn't cause the illness, of course, but God is in the illness. Indeed, God may appear for the first time because of the illness. Illness, it is said, is the Western form of meditation. Why? Because the illness gets us to reflect on God, which we might not do without the illness.

When we fall in love, it's grace. When we marry, it's grace. When we get promoted, it's grace. When we get a good grade, it's grace. "What have you that you did not receive?" Paul asked the Corinthians (1 Cor. 4:7). Nothing.

The love of our life dropped into our life. We happened to meet our spouse because the random events of our separate lives happened to put us in the same place at the same time. We got promoted because we happened to be born to parents who got us a good education.

Of course, we could say that everything that happens to us is luck.

It's bad luck to get sick, good luck to get promoted. Why bring grace into it? Because with grace we get more life. Pure greed throws us toward the divine dimension. Grace brings us over.

Saint Augustine was one of the best and the brightest. He rose through the ranks until he won a coveted professorship. Soon he was asked to give an oration in honor of the emperor. On his way to give it he met a beggar in the streets who appeared to be happier than he.

"I, on my way to this important occasion," he wrote in his famous *Confessions,* "was miserable and anxious. He, with nothing to do and no one to impress, was serenely happy. . . . I was cleverer than he was, true, but he was happier than I was."

It proved to be one of those chance events in life that turned his thinking from luck to grace. Meeting the beggar was more than chance. It was grace. And what did grace bring? More life. It brought happiness. Are we happy? Are the chance events of life adding up to happiness?

In St. Augustine's case, events added up to happiness when they added up to grace. He had led a dissolute, unhappy life shunning grace. But grace was adding up events all the time. Once they had tipped the scales, he became fully alive. Soon he was rocketing to fame as one of the leading thinkers of the Western world. A happy one, too.

My hope is that you will discover in these pages practical ways for grace to make you fully alive and absurdly happy. Dip in wherever a title catches your attention. It could be your listening point, the place where you hear God's call and are transformed by grace, God in action. The very fact that this book is in your hands now is itself sheer grace.

HOW TO EXPERIENCE GRACE
THE TRIGGER

Moses was keeping the flock.

EXODUS 3:1

One of the surprising things about the Bible is the unsurprising lives led by so many of the Bible people. They were just plain folks like most of us. They led perfectly normal, average lives. Gideon was a farmer, Isaiah a priest, Jeremiah a youth, Peter a businessman, Matthew an Internal Revenue agent.

Moses was a small businessman, minding his own business, doing his job, "keeping the flock," leading a normal, average life when the bush burned (Exod. 3:2). That says a lot. One of the conditions of the religious life, it seems, is that there are no conditions.

All we have to do to experience grace is simply to go about business as usual, doing our jobs, leading our normal, average lives. Gideon went about his farming, Isaiah his priesting, Jeremiah his teenaging, Peter his fishing business. They were doing nothing out of the ordinary when they were surprised by grace.

So often we feel we have to have a mountaintop experience to be religious. We'll experience God when we cry at a wedding or get a promotion or get into the college of our choice or have a date with the boy or girl of our dreams.

Or we feel we need a Death Valley experience to understand grace. We need to cry at a funeral or go through the loss of a job or mentor or friend or the nightmare of alcoholism or drug addiction.

But here was Moses simply going about his life, plodding along as most of us do from day to day, leading a perfectly normal, happy life with his wife and son and family and friends. Experiencing grace begins in a most unsurprising way. It is simply a matter of being who we are. As I heard a man joke, "I'm just a narrow-minded businessman." Fine. That's all he needs to experience God.

Then the outside trigger comes. It came for James and John when a man walked along a beach and said, "Follow me." It came for Gideon as he worked in his field. It came for Moses when an extraordinary bush interrupted his ordinary life. Note that the bush interrupted him. He didn't interrupt his life for it. There wasn't anything voluntary about it. It was all grace.

Grace is something that happens to us. It is not something we cause to happen. An interruption, perhaps, as we go about our unsurprising lives.

PRAYER

Help me notice when something begins to burn. Amen.

HOW TO EXPERIENCE GRACE
THE FLIP

[Paul] who once persecuted us is now preaching the
faith he once tried to destroy.

GALATIANS 1:23

One way you know it's grace is when you find yourself doing something you wouldn't normally do.
Paul found himself converted from persecutor to evangel-
ist. His life had taken a 180-degree turn. God, he said,
"had called me through his grace" (Gal. 1:15).

A man told me he was going back to all the people he
had wronged over the last twenty years. "The reception,"
he said, "has been tremendous." It was not something he

would normally have done. But God had reached him through his experiences with Alcoholics Anonymous, and his life had taken a 180-degree turn.

When we realize that the way we've been running our life isn't working, sometimes we notice something else: it is God, arriving. No matter how low we may have sunk, when we hit rock bottom, we hit rock. "This deep dread and night," the Trappist monk Thomas Merton wrote, "must then be seen for what it is: not as punishment, but as purification and as grace. Indeed it is a great gift of God, for it is the precise point of our encounter with his fullness" (Thomas Merton, *Contemplative Prayer* [New York: Random House, 1969], 79).

Is it any wonder that the word the first Christians used for *grace* was also a word they used for *gift*? The gift of grace abounds (Rom. 5:15). It multiplies (2 Cor. 4:15). It is beyond expectation (Eph. 2:7). It is "good measure, pressed down, shaken together, running over" (Luke 6:38).

"Where have I been all my life?" a man, who had just received the gift of grace, asked. "You couldn't be where you are," another man said, "if you hadn't been where you were." Everything that happens to us is bringing grace. When the gift of grace is given, we are surprised to find ourselves, like Paul, spreading the gospel, in whatever language is appropriate for us.

I doubt if my friend from AA ever used the words *God*

or *grace* when he went back to those he had wronged. But, like the apostle Paul, he was making a powerful witness. The people to whom he was making the witness got the point—that it was the power of grace propelling him back to them. They knew him, and they knew he wouldn't be coming to them on his own.

PRAYER

Bring me the image of one I have wronged. Then bring me courage. Amen.

HOW TO EXPERIENCE GRACE
THE BUILDUP

---

*If any want to become my followers, let them
deny themselves.*

MARK 8:34 NRSV

J esus was communicating a great truth. The riches of
the spiritual life are available only to the impoverished.
"Blessed are the poor in spirit," he said (Matt. 5:3). We
become poor in spirit when we deny ourselves.

Unfortunately, self-denial is not something we can do
on our own. The self is too much with us, the demands of
the ego too clamorous. Virtually every hour is consumed

with things we have to do, places we have to be, people we have to see. Letting go of all that is, simply, beyond us.

Therefore, whenever we find ourselves letting go, it has to be grace; it can't be us, because we won't do it. Not on our own, not voluntarily, not without help. Help comes in the form of whatever graceful event happens to us that takes us out of ourselves. It could be the call of a friend, the kiss of a spouse, the cry of a child.

We need these seemingly inconsequential events in life to set the ego aside so we can follow Christ. No one who put himself or herself first ever followed Jesus. History is full of examples of people who found themselves following Christ because a series of graceful events had enabled them to do so.

It is such events, in all their positive and negative ordinariness, that build up over time and displace the self from the center. Gradually, we find Jesus becoming more of a presence in our lives. We find ourselves associating more with other Christians. We find we can't get enough of the Bible. We find ourselves serving on the front lines for justice.

The importance of the seemingly unimportant cannot be overemphasized in the life of faith. Every event is full of grace, pregnant with God. Eventually, after each event has registered its importance, there comes a time when we find ourselves saying, "I didn't get this job; grace did." "I didn't bring this child into the world; grace did." "I didn't find my spouse; grace did."

We find ourselves following Christ only when the events of life have brought us to the point of following. We are constantly being surprised by grace.

PRAYER

When I find myself following Christ, may I realize it is you who has led me to follow. Amen.

HOW TO BECOME FULLY ALIVE
THE FALL

The LORD God sent him forth from the garden.
GENESIS 3:23

When we experience pain, loss, resentment, anger, fear, frustration, guilt, or any other emotion that knocks us out of control, not only are we experiencing the emotions that Adam and Eve experienced in the "fall" of humanity but also we are beginning to rise.

Falling apart can free us from the old way of doing things. If the old way had worked, we would not be falling apart. So, there is a strong plus in the apparent minus. Our symptoms are grace's way of getting us out of thinking of ourselves as heroes and into experiencing ourselves as fully alive.

Because we can no longer cope with our depression, anxiety, and stress by the rational methods we have used all our lives, we are forced to use more imaginative solutions to problems that persist. The problems have been "given" to us to free our imaginations from being stuck in too narrow a perspective.

"For freedom Christ has set us free," a liberated Paul could write (Gal. 5:1). Jesus' way of suffering is one way our imaginations can be freed from hero worship. The thing that is causing our suffering can also be the thing that is freeing us. All it takes is to find ourselves taking seriously the images that are haunting us. When we find ourselves taking them seriously, it is grace.

It is one of the great delusions that we are self-made people. We are being remade all the time, as our various symptoms break us up and plant the seeds of new being, what Paul called the "new creation" (2 Cor. 5:17). We do not will our symptoms, and we cannot will our way out of them. But we can, hopefully, find ourselves paying attention to the tawdry and violent images our symptoms produce.

When we fall apart, it is grace's way of pushing us out of the garden. Grace is putting us back together by freeing us from the delusion that we are running our own lives.

Our fall is a "gift" because the garden is too good to leave unless we are pushed. But the way to be fully alive is to discover ourselves being sent forth from the garden by grace.

PRAYER

Help me pay attention to the images produced when I am out of control. Amen.

HOW TO BECOME FULLY ALIVE
THE OVERREACH

The LORD of hosts has a day against all that is proud and lofty.

ISAIAH 2:12

The basic issue in religion is that I make a religion of myself rather than of God. All idolatry boils down to the self. This is not to say that the self cannot be wondrous as well as idolatrous. It is only to say that the more the self makes of itself, the less it is tempted to make of God.

Call it self-actualization. Call it self-fulfillment. Call it simply growth. Whatever the name, we are all striving to be what we are capable of becoming. And that is fine, as far as it goes. The trouble is, it tends to go too far, and we are brought face-to-face with sin.

Original sin, G. K. Chesterton wrote, is the only doctrine of Christian theology that can be proved. Sin is overreaching. Overreaching is what we do as we spend all our time focusing on ourselves. We end up in idolatry and pride.

"The LORD of hosts," Isaiah wrote, "has a day against all that is proud and lofty." That day comes when we realize we cannot fulfill ourselves. We cannot actualize ourselves. We cannot become who we want to be, not on our own.

The Achilles' heel of modern psychology is that it has lost the biblical sense of sin. It has rejuvenated the myth of perfectibility. But Jesus was always putting the self down, not up. "Those who want to save their life will lose it," he said (Matt. 16:25 NRSV).

All the important people in the Bible are brought low. Grace brings them down. Whatever brings us low is grace incognito. We don't see the grace in it, of course. Not yet.

"[We] are shorn of any idolatrous confidence in self," writes Glenn Whitlock in the *Journal of Religion and Health*. "Selfhood cannot be achieved through will power. The courage to realize the potentiality of being a whole person comes from God. This courage comes from God's acceptance of [us] even though [we are] unacceptable. This acceptance is demonstrated through Jesus Christ."

Faith begins when I end. "I am nothing," Paul said (2 Cor. 12:11). "I...am but dust and ashes," Abraham said (Gen. 18:27). "I despise myself," Job said (Job 42:6). Grace was able to use such people because they were no longer proud and lofty. Indeed, when Job was proud and lofty, he had no time for God. Grace was at work on Job, Paul, and Abraham to bring them fully alive.

PRAYER

Help me learn my limits through my teacher, grace.
Amen.

HOW TO BECOME FULLY ALIVE
THE PASSIVE

Christ Jesus has made me his own.

PHILIPPIANS 3:12

The Bible opens a new dimension. We enter a world in which the passive supplants the active. "I chose David," God says (1 Kings 8:16). David didn't choose God. "I chose Israel," God says through Ezekiel (Ezek. 20:5). "I chose you," Jesus says to his disciples (John 15:16). "Christ Jesus," Paul writes, "has made me his own."

The passive is a dimension we never enter on our own.

We are activists. We are like Paul, the disciples, David, the Israelites. But what they learned was that their activism wasn't enough.

David had a man killed in order to get the man's wife. Paul had Christians thrown into jail. The disciples and Israelites were constantly taking things into their own hands.

It is only when grace entered their lives that such people came fully alive. Grace had been there all along, of course; but they had not known it, because they were so intent on pursuing their own activist agendas.

Consequently, their activism had to bring them to the point where grace could break them through to the passive side of who they were, where things were done through them, not by them.

When we are running things, we don't need grace. But when our running of things turns out badly, grace gains an entry point. Of course, grace could gain an entry point at any time, but often grace doesn't gain entry until our activism plays itself out.

Christ Jesus did not make Paul "his own" until Paul had jailed hundreds of Christians and voted for their executions. "When they were put to death I cast my vote against them" (Acts 26:10). His activism was appalling.

It took an intervention by Nathan to acquaint the activist, David, with the appalling nature of what he had done. Only then was David able to say, "I have sinned against the LORD" (2 Sam. 12:13). Grace in the form of Nathan appeared too late to save a life, but that is the way it often has to be with activist agendas, even though grace has been struggling all along to make its appearance.

Apparently, we have to be thrown onto our passive side. We do not go voluntarily. "The kingdom of God is preached," Jesus said, "and every one enters it violently" (Luke 16:16).

PRAYER

May the events of my life be giving you an opening.
Amen.

HOW TO BECOME FULLY ALIVE
THE WAR

I delight in the law of God, in my inmost self.

ROMANS 7:22

L et's assume that we are not all we could be. One would be brash indeed to assume the opposite. We have only to look at how it has been in our lives—how we have not worked to capacity, how we have taken wrong turns, made our share of mistakes.

Let us also assume that there is something in us urging us to be more than we have been, to come over into that broad, good place of self-discovery where we are fully functioning, leading happy, productive lives. "The glory of God," said Irenaeus, an early Christian, "is a person fully alive."

Between the old self and the new self there appears to be an irreconcilable conflict. The classical expression of this conflict is found in St. Paul, who called it a "war." "I delight in the law of God, in my inmost self," he wrote, "but I see . . . another law at war with the law of my mind and making me captive to the law of sin" (Rom. 7:22-23).

The question then becomes, how do we win the war? How does the new self complement the old? "A house divided against itself cannot stand," Lincoln quoted Jesus (Mark 3:25). Historically, there have been two ways to answer those questions—on our own or with help. The Bible takes the route of "with help." Much of the time we take the route of "on our own."

We pull out all the stops. We take the assignments. We accept the challenges. We meet the tests. We get through school. We go to college. We land a good job. We get married, have children, buy a house. We feel that we are fully alive. Then a child ends up on drugs. Or we lose our job. Or our health declines. Or we take the wrong turn. That's when we begin to think there may be another way.

Or we could have thought this way long before. We don't have to have a crisis to begin thinking about God. We can come to God through the good experiences of life as well as the bad.

Maybe when we got married we gave the credit to God for bringing our loved one into our life. Maybe when we got that first job, or our first child. Maybe when we stepped outside one morning into the beauty of spring.

The first thing that has to go if we are to be fully alive is the old self, which goes it alone. The old self has to be complemented by our new self, the one Paul called his "inmost" self, the one that is surprised by grace. Grace, working through the events of life, is doing the complementing and gradually making us fully alive.

PRAYER

Help me glorify you by becoming fully alive. Amen.

HOW TO HANDLE
ADDICTION

The truth will make you free.

JOHN 8:32

Many of our struggles, including our addictions, can be gifts bringing us God. How can that be? Addiction shows us we are powerless. Maybe we are addicted to perfection and are powerless to relax and let things be. Or maybe we are addicted to success and are powerless over ambition.

Instead, though, of dealing directly with our addictions, we tend to project them onto others. Jesus was ar-

22

rested, scourged, and killed by people who did not face their addiction to power. The Holocaust happened because the Nazis were addicted to their Aryanism. Our children are victimized, even brutalized, because we will not deal with our addiction to impatience.

Often it takes a crisis to show us we are powerless. We fail at work; a child falls ill; the doctor tells us we will die if we continue to drink.

Our powerlessness can be God's road to power. God arrives in our realization that we are addicted. Grace gives us an image of the powerless Jesus on the cross. Somehow that can free us. "If the Son makes you free," he said, "you will be free indeed" (John 8:36). He was speaking of our slavery to sin. "If you continue in my word, . . . you will know the truth, and the truth will make you free" (John 8:31-32).

The key, then, to overcoming addiction is to find ourselves making Christ our "addiction." It is to find ourselves substituting slavery to him for slavery to sin. The first Christians called themselves "slaves of Christ" (Phil. 1:1). Most translations prefer the euphemism "servant," but the Greek is "slave." They used such language to demonstrate that slavery to the Master had superseded slavery to sin, to any form of addiction that had once been the most important thing in a person's life.

Of course, we cannot simply decide to become slaves of the Master. Our addictions are too powerful. That is why we may need grace in the form of a crisis to do it for us. An upheaval may be the only way to get an image of Jesus so powerful that it can overpower the image of the next drink or of the next rung on the ladder of success.

PRAYER

I pray for the gift of such an image now. Amen.

HOW TO KEEP THE
FAITH ALIVE

---

*Where two or three are gathered in my name, there
am I.*

MATTHEW 18:20

There are many things we can do alone, but Christianity is not one of them. A Christian alone is a contradiction in terms. "Where two or three are gathered in my name," Jesus said, "there am I in the midst of them."

The writer of Hebrews takes it a step further. "We are surrounded," he writes, "by so great a cloud of witnesses" (Heb. 12:1). He was thinking of all who were faithful, going as far back as Abel, Enoch, Noah, and Abraham. We stand on the shoulders of giants, as Isaac Newton said in another context, and if it weren't for their shoulders, we wouldn't be standing at all.

The collectivity of faith is also what keeps faith alive in each church. In some churches, as many as four generations will be together on Sunday. No other social institution has so many people of so many ages in one place at one time every week. And even the church cemeteries represent the generations who have preceded the current four. We can't take communion alone. We can't be baptized alone. They are the two central acts of the Christian faith. By their very nature they are corporate, not individual. We can worship alone, of course, in meditation and prayer, as Jesus did; but for these two central acts, we need the worshiping community.

Jesus gathered twelve disciples and then more disciples until there were one hundred twenty (Acts 1:15). There is something in the power of the collective that is missing in the power of the individual. All Paul's letters are to churches. The first Christians knew that without one another their new faith had little chance.

Why are we among them? Because we have been brought by grace. We don't go to church; we are brought to church. How do we know? Because we haven't gone on our own. The enticement of a day off is too much. So when we do go, it has to be grace; it can't be us. "No one can come to me," Jesus said, "unless drawn by the Father who sent me" (John 6:44 NRSV).

PRAYER

Help me recognize how much I need other Christians.
Amen.

HOW TO HEAR GOD
SPEAK

The LORD roars from Zion.

AMOS 1:2

A mos heard God because he was in position to hear God. He was at a listening point. We can be, too. For one thing, Amos was alone. Shepherds did their herding alone. Most of us rarely take time to be alone. We go down the street with a phone in our ear. We turn the car radio on. The TV blares until bedtime.

Amos was outside, in nature. Many speak of how close they feel to God in nature. Amos was no exception.

Being out in nature stimulated his theological imagination. "The LORD God roars from Zion, . . . the pastures of the shepherds mourn, and the top of Carmel withers."

Amos lived in a time of crisis. Israel in 760 B.C. was in chaos. The rich were getting richer while the poor were getting poorer, as happens all too often in America. People were being sold into slavery. Small farmers were being dispossessed. The courts were dishonest. The professional prophets were silent, as religious leaders all too often are. Amos had no special theological training, like most of us. He was not a member of the prophetic guild. Yet he was the first prophet whose prophecies were preserved as a separate book.

Amos was in position to hear God speak because grace had positioned him. It was pure grace that he lived where and when he did. "It was from such peasant homes," writes a scholar, "that many of Israel's greatest leaders came. . . . It was in peasant homes as his that the true culture and faith of Israel were preserved from generation to generation."

Alone, in nature, in a time of crisis, with no special theological training, but brought up in the faith, we, too, can find ourselves at a listening point. If God could speak to Amos, why not to us?

PRAYER

Help me realize you could be speaking to me now. Amen.

HOW TO HANDLE ANXIETY

Cast all your anxieties on him, for he cares about you.

1 PETER 5:7

We all have things about which we are anxious. Among them are our children, mortgage, job, parents, and health. But there is a difference between concern and anxiety. These are all things for which we should be properly concerned. There is some question, however, whether we should be anxious about them.

"Take heed to yourselves," Jesus said, "lest your hearts be weighed down with ... [the] cares of this life" (Luke 21:34). When legitimate concerns begin to weigh us

30

down, that is when we begin to experience anxiety. Jesus spoke of anxiety using another metaphor: There "are those," he said, "who hear the word, but the cares of the world...enter in and choke the word" (Mark 4:18-19). The word *anxiety* comes from the root for "strangle." We can always tell how anxious we are by how fast we are breathing.

Peter had every reason to be anxious. He was writing at the time of Nero's persecution of the Christians. He tells of their being "tested by fire" (1 Pet. 1:7). But he also gives those he is writing to an antidote to anxiety. "Cast all your anxieties on him," he writes, referring to God, "for he cares about you."

Easier said than done, to be sure. But that is why we have one another. Christians remind one another that God cares. "My grace," Paul heard God say in his illness, "is sufficient for you" (2 Cor. 12:9). "Do not be anxious about your life," Jesus said, "but seek first his kingdom and his righteousness" (Matt. 6:25, 33).

Most of us have two types of anxiety. One is about the past, which goes by such names as guilt, grief, regret, remorse. All are perfectly natural, and all tend to weigh us down from time to time and speed up our breathing. There is also anxiety about the future, which goes by such names as worry, stress, ambition, fear. Either way, past or future, anxiety takes us out of the present.

So how do we "cast our anxieties" on God? Grace

moves us to meditate, which is something we would never do on our own. We find ourselves meditating. We may lose the present in anxiety, but we never lose the presence—if, that is, we are anxious enough to find ourselves moved to meditate. Meditating on one phrase at a time from the Lord's Prayer is one way to do it. A single word like *Jesus* is another way. We say the first syllable as we inhale and the second as we exhale.

Peter and the other first Christians were ultimately able to win out over the persecutions because they found themselves casting their anxieties on God. The blood of the martyrs, as the old saying goes, became the seed of the church.

PRAYER

Help me practice your presence each day so that when I am most anxious you will be most present. Amen.

HOW TO BELIEVE

Faith is the assurance of things hoped for.

HEBREWS 11:1

How can we have faith like that? *Assurance* can also be translated "reality." "Faith is the reality of things hoped for."

Just as 1 Corinthians 13 is the great love chapter in the Bible, so Hebrews 11 is the great faith chapter. It reminds us that faith is proved by works. The word *faith* is never used in Genesis or Exodus. It doesn't have to be. The faith is in the act.

"By faith Abel offered" (Heb. 11:4). "By faith

Noah...constructed" (Heb. 11:7). "By faith Abraham obeyed" (Heb. 11:8). "By faith Sarah...considered" (Heb. 11:11). "By faith Isaac invoked" (Heb. 11:20). "By faith Jacob...blessed" (Heb. 11:21).

The faith is in the works. How we believe is evident in how we behave. "They'll know we are Christians by our love," is the refrain of a popular song. Exactly.

Saint Augustine led a dissolute life until his mid-thirties. Then one day he heard some children outside his window. Ordinarily, he would not have given them another thought. But this was no ordinary time. This was grace. "Take, read; take, read" was the refrain of a game they were playing. Inspired by grace, he picked up the nearest book, a Bible, and opened it. His eye fell on Romans 13, the last paragraph: "Let us conduct ourselves becomingly as in the day, not in reveling and drunkenness, not in debauchery and licentiousness, not in quarreling and jealousy. But put on the Lord Jesus Christ." (Rom. 13:13-14). It changed his life. From then on his works proved his faith. The debauchee became a saint.

Would that faith were so easily gotten, we say. But it can be. "At the right time Christ died for [us]," Paul wrote (Rom. 5:6). He should know. His timing had been off for years. Then suddenly it was on as he rode to Damascus to arrest Christians. "I saw...a light from heaven" (Acts 26:13). It was grace.

Faith comes when we are ready. We are being readied

by grace. We can tell it is faith when we are surprised by our new behavior.

PRAYER

May I be surprised by something I find myself doing today.
Amen.

HOW TO IDENTIFY GRACE

[Barnabas] . . . saw the grace of God.

ACTS 11:23

The Christian's job is to identify grace in others. Barnabas did it exceptionally well. He saw grace where even Paul did not. The young man, John Mark, had deserted Paul and Barnabas on an earlier trip. So Paul did not want to take him on a new one. But Barnabas would not desert the deserter. "Barnabas took Mark with him and sailed away to Cyprus" (Acts 15:39).

Our job is to stay with others until they recognize God and to help them see the grace we see. "The priesthood of all believers" means that each of us is a priest for others. The priest's job is to identify grace. How does he or she do that? By staying with the other person.

Barnabas stayed with the people in Antioch "for a whole year" (Acts 11:26). He even went to Tarsus to hunt for Paul to bring him back to Antioch to help. He would not give up on his job of identifying grace. "I will be with you," he was saying by his actions, "until you can see what God is doing in your life. And I will love you just as you are, so you can see it."

One way to help another see grace is to love persistently. That is what Barnabas was doing. He was helping others to see the grace in their lives by standing by them "for a whole year."

Our calling as Christians is to stand by others until they see God in their everyday lives. We are not to desert them but to challenge them to stand by others until they, in turn, see God. When we find ourselves heeding our call, it is grace.

If Barnabas and others like him had not stood by other Christians in the first century, there would be no Christians in the twenty-first century.

PRAYER

Help me encourage others until they see you. Amen.

HOW TO LIVE IN THE
PRESENT

This night your soul is required of you.

LUKE 12:20

The man to whom God said, "This night your soul is required of you," was not ready to die because, in Jesus' words, he was not "rich toward God" (Luke 12:21). He was too busy building up his retirement account so he could take his ease, eat, drink, and be merry (Luke 12:19).

The only possible antidote to dying tonight is living today. As a cancer patient once said to me, "Bob, live every moment." Living in the present is how we are rich toward God. We are rich because we are living in the presence. We are no longer bound to the past, with guilt or regret, or to the future with anxiety or fear. We are free to live now. Grace is what frees us.

Of course, living now is not all that easy. It is one of the hardest things to do in life. That is why we need help. Guilt, regret, anxiety, fear are not emotions we can handle on our own. Grace enables us to handle them and live now.

One way we know we are rich toward God is by the amount of joy in our lives. A joyless Christian is a contradiction in terms. The early Christians sang hymns on their way to execution. Talk about living now! Talk about being rich toward God!

One of the best proofs of God's existence is joy in adversity. Witness again the early Christians. "Count it all joy," one wrote, "when you meet various trials" (James 1:2). "We rejoice in our sufferings," Paul wrote (Rom. 5:3). To Christians under threat of death, Peter wrote: "You ... rejoice with unutterable and exalted joy" (1 Pet. 1:8).

They had learned how to live now, and they had learned it from Jesus. "I have learned the secret," Paul was to write from jail. "I can do all things in him who strengthens me" (Phil. 4:12-13).

So can we.

PRAYER

Help me live so much in the now that joy is a way of life.
Amen.

HOW TO READ THE BIBLE

*Mary kept all these things, pondering them in
her heart.*

LUKE 2:19

There are many things we can read fast, but the Bible
is not one of them. If we have read more than a few
verses and haven't pondered anything, then we are probably going too fast. Reading the Bible like a book is perhaps the single biggest mistake we can make with the
Bible.

We can't begin to observe everything going on in the
sacred space of the Bible if we read faster than a few
words, phrases, or sentences a minute. I was in a small

group reading the Gospel of John once a week. We discovered it took us an average of five weeks per chapter.

"Be still, and know that I am God" (Ps. 46:10). Go slow, and know. Dawdle. Go down the side roads. Take in everything. Stop often. Get the image of a walk with a two-year-old, where everything is new.

We stop when a word, phrase, image, or feeling arrests us. We call being arrested, grace. The pondering psalm begins with the simple sentence, "Praise the Lord" (Ps. 111:1). We might find ourselves stopping right there, struck, as Mary was at Jesus' birth, by all the things in life for which to praise the Lord. She "kept all these things, pondering them in her heart."

Then we carry into our day or night the word, phrase, thought, image, feeling that caught our attention. We find ourselves laying it as a template on everything we do. A template is a metal cut-out used as a guide in replication, a cookie-cutter. We contemplate what grace has brought to our attention.

We ponder the "works of the Lord" as an overlay on everything we do. We see our child as a work of the Lord, and our spouse, our job, our fellow employees, our food. I heard a rabbi tell a group of Christians that Jews try to see everything during the day as a work of the Lord, right down to the intimate details. The Word of God works as a template on our nights, too, as we read it before going to sleep, where it mingles with the unconscious and works its way into our dreams, converting the riot of images from the day into a new sacred space.

PRAYER

Help me take time to ponder your Word. Amen.

HOW TO CONTEMPLATE
THE BIBLE

Great are the works of the Lord; they are pondered
by all who delight in them.

PSALM 111:2 NRSV

What does it mean to ponder? It means to seek out the inner meaning, to contemplate, ruminate. As a cow chews its cud, so we chew on a Bible passage that catches our attention. Ezekiel was told to eat the divine words in the form of a scroll (Ezek. 2:8).

The word *contemplate* comes from the Latin *templum,* an open space marked out for observation by ancient priests called augurs, a place reserved, sacred, holy. The priest would observe what was going on in this sacred space in order to divine the intentions of the gods and so be able to issue an augury, an announcement about the future.

The Bible is a sacred space, or temple, cut out from all other spaces for our observation, our contemplation, our pondering. But why pay attention to the Bible? What is the motivation for entering its sacred space?

"The word of God is living and active," a Bible writer writes, "sharper than any two-edged sword, piercing to the division of soul and spirit, of joints and marrow, and discerning the thoughts and intentions of the heart. And before him no creature is hidden, but all are open and laid bare to the eyes of him with whom we have to do" (Heb. 4:12-13).

The Bible lays us bare. That is the motivation for pulling it off the shelf. It gets us down to the inner core of who we are, where the truth about ourselves resides, where we stand alone before God, the one "to whom we must render an account" (Heb. 4:13 NRSV). Grace is behind this motivation to be laid bare. We would never seek to be laid bare on our own. How do we know? Because we hardly ever read the Bible on our own.

The Bible reminds us that we are not to fritter our lives away on not being fully alive. It reminds us to ponder "the works of the Lord" to get more out of life. Without the

Bible, we might never ponder them. Without the Bible, we might never find ourselves moved into sacred space, because all space would be secular, one-dimensional, human only.

Once in the Bible, however, we might be surprised to see ourselves as one of the "works of the Lord." We discover right in the first chapter that we are made in the image of God (Gen. 1:26). That's enough right there to get our attention. Surely, such an image lays us bare. We have to answer for how we are carrying it. But we wouldn't find ourselves answering if grace had not gotten us into the Bible in the first place.

PRAYER

May I find myself every day in the sacred space of your Word.
Amen.

HOW TO HANDLE A
PROBLEM

I despise myself, / and repent in dust and ashes.

JOB 42:6

A man had a problem with alcohol. He did everything he could on his own to solve it. Finally, when he saw that all his own hard work wouldn't get him to stop, he went to his doctor. After discussing his problem the doctor said, "Get your coat on. We're going for a ride."

They went to the detox unit at a local hospital. The man was shocked by what he saw. When they returned to the doctor's office and finished the physical exam, the man suddenly found himself on his knees in the examining room when the doctor had left, confessing his need to Christ. At that moment, Christ came into his life, and he never had another drink.

"I believe in hard work," my friend said to me, "but I also believe in miracles." It was the hard work on his problem that brought him to the point where he could see that his own work wouldn't work. Then the miracle occurred, and he found himself confessing his inability to handle his problem on his own. At the point of the death of his old life, he was born again into a new one. Ever after, he would refer to his alcoholism as a gift.

Job was a good man, but he was arrogant. He knew he was a good man. He did everything right. He even believed in God right. But he had not yet confessed. So God was going to have to bring him to his knees. With the longest speech by God in the Bible, Job 38-41, God steamrolls Job with sarcasm. It is then that Job finds himself saying, "I despise myself, / and repent in dust and ashes."

What personal problem are we trying to solve on our own? Have we discovered that it is so large we can't solve it on our own? That discovery is grace. Has that discovery dropped us to our knees in confession, and has our confession brought God? And can we now call our problem a gift because it has brought our God?

As Abraham Lincoln, who had his share of problems, said: "Man is tallest on his knees."

PRAYER

Help me see my problem as a gift bringing me to you. Amen.

HOW TO ACCESS GOD

The sacrifice acceptable to God is a broken spirit.

PSALM 51:17

One way to access God is through brokenness. A psalmist gained such access through an experience of guilt. "I know my transgressions/," he wrote, "and my sin is ever before me" (Ps. 51:1).

His experience of brokenness released a torrent of images. "Wash...cleanse...purge...fill...blot...cast." It was as if the shattering of his ego by guilt had stimulated his creativity. It had also stimulated his awareness of God. All the images are addressed to God. The gift of his brokenness was that it was bringing him God.

It is no accident that the two supreme images in the Bible are images of brokenness. In the Old Testament it is the image of the Suffering Servant in Isaiah 53, and in the New Testament it is the image of Jesus on the cross.

There is something about being broken that moves us into another dimension. It must have to do with our no longer being in control. When we are not in control, God can be.

Someone gave me a little paperback book by Ole Hallesby entitled simply *Prayer*. The entire book revolves around one word, *helpless*. We never really pray, Hallesby says, until we are helpless. "All religion," William James wrote, "begins in a cry for help."

Until we are helpless, we don't need God. Until we are broken, we won't access God, at least not in the kind of depth the psalmist is talking about. "The sacrifice acceptable to God," he says, "is a broken spirit."

God was able to break through to the psalmist because the psalmist found himself being honest about his brokenness. Grace was what enabled him to be honest. Now he could face his guilt, admit it, and then let it do whatever it had to do.

Normally, we would not let guilt be. We would not allow ourselves to be helpless before it. We would bury it in alcohol or "workahol" or take it out on others. But the wisdom of the psalm is that, if we find ourselves letting our guilt be, it is grace finding us. The way is now clear for God to arrive through the very images of the guilt itself, such as the face of the one whom we have wronged.

PRAYER

Help me allow my guilt to lead me to you. Amen.

HOW TO BE HAPPY

Those who lose their life for my sake will find it.

MATTHEW 16:25 NRSV

Do we feel stressed, uneasy, at odds with ourselves? Do we feel we're in a civil war, in inner conflict? "I'm running here, I'm running there," someone said, "I'm always on the go." And it was said as though life were a constant torment.

There is an antidote to such stress. It's called finding ourselves by losing ourselves, and it comes straight from Jesus: "Those who lose their life for my sake will find it."

Losing ourselves is the opposite of how we normally

think of finding happiness. Normally, we think we find happiness by pursuing it. But Jesus is saying that happiness finds us as we find ourselves lost in him.

Isn't that how it works in life? We find ourselves by losing ourselves in causes greater than ourselves. As disciples, our cause could be peace, justice, a profitable company, a happy home, a more attractive community, or all the above.

"I have discovered," Abraham Lincoln said, "that people are about as happy as they make up their minds to be." He said it during his attempt to save the country, a big cause if ever there was one. But he also said it as a result of his many attempts to save himself from his frequent bouts of melancholy. Once when he was on the legal circuit, he stayed up all night staring into the fire, brooding.

Happiness may be elusive, but if grace can get us losing ourselves in something greater than ourselves, we have a chance at it.

PRAYER

Help me lose myself in something bigger than myself because I am a disciple. Amen.

HOW TO HEAR A CALL

Whom shall I send, and who will go for us?
ISAIAH 6:8

Though we'd like to think of our jobs as calls, mostly our jobs are just jobs. Our call will come when we are ready.

One form that grace can take is that of the organic call. It fits. It's who we are. We feel that it is what we were meant to do. "It's me," we say. "I'm having fun. I lose track of time." I had a professor who took the steps two at a time to get to his office every morning.

Isaiah was in a worship service when his call came.

The events of his life had brought him to a listening point. "Whom shall I send," he heard God say, "and who will go for us?" "Here am I!" Isaiah found himself responding. "Send me." Isaiah heard God repeatedly during his career as a prophet. We may hear God calling us to a different career—or to stay in the same career.

When will our call come? Who knows? William Penn had just been converted to Quakerism. It was the custom for a British aristocrat to wear his sword. Penn went to the Quaker leader, George Fox, and asked him, "When should I take off my sword?" "When you are ready," Fox replied.

Our calls are coming all the time. We just aren't always ready to hear them. Fortunately, we are being readied all the time. Grace is using the events of life to ready us. Everything we do, everything that happens to us, is moving us toward a listening point where, at last, we can hear God call.

There can be several such listening points. A call need not be once and for all. It can be, but it doesn't have to be. Our call could change. It could be affirmed. It could be added to. Life continues, which means grace could once again bring us to a listening point.

But how do we know it is God calling and not just something we want to do? The two need not be mutually exclusive. We know it's a call by giving it St. Paul's test, what he called the "fruit of the Spirit" (Gal. 5:22). If we have more of the following in life, we just may be hearing—and obeying—God's call: "love, joy, peace, patience, kindness, goodness, faithfulness, gentleness, self-control."

"How do I know it's a call?" a teenager asked her parish priest. "You know it's a call," he replied, "by your joy." She spread that joy around the world as Mother Teresa.

PRAYER

May I find myself every day experiencing more love, joy, and peace. Amen.

HOW TO HEAR A CALL
THAT DOESN'T "FIT"

Who am I that I should go?

EXODUS 3:11

A call may not always fit, at least not on first hearing. Moses was doing just fine herding his father-in-law's sheep. He had a wife and child and a secure job. The last thing he needed was to have all that changed. "Who am I that I should go?" he asks at the burning bush. How could he be the one to lead the Israelites out of Egypt?

Your call may be the very thing you feel least equipped to do.

Paul had devoted his entire life to hounding Christians. "I persecuted this Way to the death," he said, "binding and delivering to prison both men and women" (Acts 22:4). Then the call came—to do something completely different, for which he had no apparent qualifications. "Saul, Saul," he heard Jesus saying, "why do you persecute me?" (Acts 9:4)

There is a startling phrase in the story of Jesus' temptations. "Then Jesus was led up by the Spirit...to be tempted" (Matt. 4:1). The Spirit was in control even when Jesus was being tempted to call something a call when it wasn't. The devil can be in what appears to be most organic for us. Jesus was tempted by economic, political, and magical power when his call was actually to spiritual power. His temptations were his very real resistance to his true call.

The thing we can do best may not be the best thing we can do. It takes a call to get us to do the best thing because we would never do it on our own. Without a call, Moses would never have left the security of home and job to do something he knew he couldn't do.

When we find ourselves doing something we would never have done on our own, it could be God calling. If that is the way it was for person after person in the Bible, then that is the way it can be for us. Grace never rests.

PRAYER

What is it I am resisting? Amen.

HOW TO HEAR A CALL
THAT UNSETTLES US

So Abram went, as the LORD had told him.

GENESIS 12:4

One way we may know we're being called is if we're unsettled. God's call to Abraham meant having to leave home, job, friends, and country. God's call turned Paul's life upside down. Once Moses answered God's call, he was no longer vice president of his father-in-law's livestock company.

What bothers us so much that we can't eat or sleep? It could be God calling. For verification we may find ourselves drawn by grace to the Bible. It can speak to us as never before. The circumstances of life have placed us in position to hear. We may find ourselves identifying with Abraham. For the ancient Hebrews, the faith was in the behavior more than in the belief. Abraham left for the promised land. "He went out, not knowing where he was to go" (Heb. 11:8). The faith was in the act, no matter how unsettling.

The calling is in the going. The hearing is in the doing. We can hardly believe it, but we find ourselves doing it. We don't know how things will turn out, yet we find ourselves on our way. We are leaving the safe for the bold, the easy for the unsettled. It has to be grace. We wouldn't do any of this on our own.

"Then the LORD appeared to Abram" (Gen. 12:7). God did not appear until faith became act and belief became behavior. It is here that God gives Abraham the tremendous promise: "To your descendants I will give this land" (Gen. 12:7).

What is Abraham's response? "So he built there an altar to the LORD" (Gen. 12:7). This was how he would commemorate the appearance of God in his life. We, too, can build an "altar" at home or at work, a sacred space where we can affirm God's appearance in the Bible and prayer. I dropped in on a friend at work. I was surprised to see a Bible on his desk.

PRAYER

Why am I feeling unsettled? Amen.

HOW TO OBEY CHRIST'S
COMMANDS

Woe to you Pharisees!

LUKE 11:43

We don't obey Christ's commands because there is anything in it for us. We obey them because they are Christ's commands. That is the sole motivation. There is nothing prudential about it. We obey them not because they will make us happier, wealthier, or more successful or give us more peace of mind or make us better persons. We obey them simply because they are Christ's commands.

Of course, such "blind" obedience is totally insufficient

motivation for most of us. Consequently, whenever we find ourselves obeying any of Christ's commands, it has to be grace moving us to obey. We can't obey on our own. We can take zero credit when it comes to obeying Christ's commands. All the credit is God's; none can be ours.

If we take any credit, the religious game is up. This is one area of life where we get no credit. The reason Jesus denounced the Pharisees so severely was that they had to have credit for obeying the 613 rules of their religion. They did it. They were the ones who could measure up. No one else could "do" the Jewish religion as well as they could. Hence their notorious judgmentalism. Their name even means "the separated ones."

"Woe to you Pharisees! for you love the best seat in the synagogues and salutations in the market places." Why did they love the best seat? Because they were the best people, the only ones who were able to keep all the laws, obey all the orders, respond to all the commands. They were the ones. They did it. They motivated themselves. God didn't.

We can't motivate ourselves to obey Christ's commands. They are too tough. The bar is too high. We can't jump over it on our own.

Can't is arguably the most important word in the Bible. Why? Because it throws us off our own resources and onto God's, which is precisely what has to happen to self-reliant, can-do, narcissistic, pharisaical types who think they can succeed in religion just as they have succeeded in life. Jesus knew that. The divinity was in the impossibility of the commands.

So, when we find ourselves turning the other cheek, loving our enemies, praying for those who persecute us, it is all grace, no us. In that moment, God has appeared in our lives. Our lifelong quest for God is over. God has arrived in our sudden, startling obedience.

PRAYER

Whenever I obey Christ's command, remind me you are enabling me to do so. Amen.

HOW TO HANDLE
CATASTROPHE

For God so loved the world that he gave his only Son.

JOHN 3:16

We have heard John 3:16 since childhood, but keeping it fresh in adversity is another matter. John's great statement reminds us of God's powerful love, "For God so loved the world that he gave his only Son." With that kind of love, we can handle anything.

It's presumptuous, however, to say to someone in the midst of a catastrophic event, "You can handle anything." In that moment, that person feels crushed. "We were so utterly, unbearably crushed," Paul wrote, "that we despaired of life itself" (2 Cor. 1:8). But the unconditional love of God in Jesus Christ sustained him. No catastrophe is too great if we are able to experience this love.

How do we experience it? One way is in the form of a small group. Once or twice a month, six to ten people get together in homes to study the Bible, share experiences, and serve in a mission project. The small group is a ritual that works. Many such groups have been meeting regularly for years. They discover an intimacy and accountability in matters of faith they had never known before. They experience the unconditional love of God in Jesus Christ right in their own living rooms.

I have been in several such groups. In one, a teenager had just lost her mother in an auto accident. She left the group discussion one night and went into another room to be alone. One by one the rest of the group went to be with her. We surrounded her and held her and prayed for her. An experience like that puts vivid flesh on the tired bones of Sunday-morning intercessions.

The long-ago memorization of John 3:16 can come alive this way. Otherwise, the downward spiral into catastrophe may become all but inevitable. Before that happens, grace can lead us to join a small group.

PRAYER

May I find myself experiencing your unconditional love
in a small group. Amen.

HOW TO HAVE A
CHILDLIKE FAITH

---

*Whoever does not receive the kingdom of God like a
child shall not enter it.*

MARK 10:15

hildren are wonderful, full of wonder. "All philosophy," Plato said, "begins in wonder." If we need con-
vincing that children are wonderful, all we need to do is
walk down the street with a two-year-old. I once took a
four-year-old to Chicago's Museum of Natural History.
He was so wonderful that after three hours, I was collaps-
ing and he was pleading to see yet another exhibit.

The ancient Hebrews had the same sense of wonder: "When I look at thy heavens, the work of thy fingers, the moon and the stars which thou hast established; what is man that thou are mindful of him, and the son of man that thou dost care for him?" (Ps. 8:3-4). Those ancients, it has been said, did not take the leap of faith but the look of faith. They looked beyond what they saw. It was the same childlike motivation for what later became known as science. Scientists are wonderful, full of wonder, often childlike.

We can never quite explain reality. As we sit amazed that our dining room table is a collection of atoms and that our spouse across from us loves us, we are prime candidates for experiencing the kingdom of God.

There are only three possible attitudes about the beyond. One is the fatalistic. Fate, which has no purpose and no justice, controls the world. Another is the positivistic. The beyond does not exist, and the mere notion of it is meaningless. A third attitude is theistic. The beyond does exist and is in the hands of a God who is concerned about wonderful people.

This last attitude is only for those with a childlike sense of wonder. It is clearly a gift. Some call it grace.

PRAYER

Help me never lose my sense of wonder. Amen.

HOW TO KEEP YOUR
PLAYFULNESS

Let the children come to me.

MARK 10:14

Children are playful. It was their very playfulness that
encouraged the disciples to "rebuke" them (Mark
10:13). They didn't want the children bothering Jesus.
He saw it differently. "Let the children come to me," he
said.

Play is an end in itself. It doesn't save the world or
clean the house or put the bread on the table. Play is
what it is, nothing more. "Homo ludens" complements

"homo sapiens," which is humanity playful as well as humanity wise.

Jesus turned aside to play. Being with the children was an end in itself. It wouldn't "accomplish" anything. He had no ulterior motive. When they came into his life, he took time to be with them.

To play is to be present to what is happening to us. It is to be absorbed in the moment with no thought of what happens next. It is the opposite of looking past the person we are with in order to greet someone else. That's living in the next moment, not this one.

God is in the present. Epiphany is always now. The moment is all.

The playful perception of God in the moment is how to see God. Grace keeps us in the moment. To the child the moment is alive. The moment is all there is. Grace keeps us childlike and playful.

The problem for most of us is that the habit of conceptualizing builds up over the years as we leave childhood, and we are no longer present to the present. Thought takes precedence over feeling, and we lose the moment. Deep in thought, I lost the moon one night on my way home and had to be reminded to look.

Present-moment living is a child's gift to adults. Jesus knew its importance for faith, which is why he made an example of children. "Whoever does not receive the kingdom of God like a child," he said, "shall not enter it" (Mark 10:15).

PRAYER

Lord, help me stay more in the present so that I may experience you more. Amen.

HOW TO BE CHOSEN

The LORD your God has chosen you.
DEUTERONOMY 7:6

The LORD your God has chosen you," the Israelites are told. "You did not choose me," Jesus says to his disciples, "but I chose you" (John 15:16). The Bible was there with its announcement before we were there with our faith.

The remarkable thing is that there are no conditions for being chosen. There is nothing we have to do. "It was not because you were more in number . . . that the LORD set his love upon you," the Bible explains, "for you were the fewest of all peoples; but it is because the LORD loves you" (Deut. 7:7-8). "For God so loved the world that he gave his only begotten Son" (John 3:16 KJV).

No one in the Bible claims faith as an achievement. "Neither the one who plants nor the one who waters is anything," Paul wrote, "but only God who gives the growth" (1 Cor. 3:7 NRSV). "I am nothing," he was to say later (2 Cor. 12:11). And he said it to the affluent Corinthians, who were noted for their achievements.

Faith is not one more achievement of the heroic ego. It is something produced in the ego by grace. If we take credit for it, we lose it. Faith has to be passive in that something is done for us rather than by us. "By grace you have been saved through faith," the Bible says, "and this is not your own doing, it is the gift of God" (Eph. 2:8).

Faith is a gift, not a work. Thinking about faith this way requires a whole new mind-set. Faith is not something we do; it is something done for us. There is nothing we can do to get faith; faith has to get us, at the right moment in our lives. When is the right moment? Whenever. It could be now; it could be later. "At the right time," Paul said, "Christ died for [us]" (Rom. 5:6).

"I have a feeling about the coaxial lines of life," Augie March says in Saul Bellows's *The Adventures of Augie March*. The various lines of our lives have to come together for faith to happen. How do they come together? By simply living out our lives. Eventually, the lines of our lives come together and faith happens.

And if the lines don't come together? But they are coming together! They are coming together all the time. The very act of reading the lines on this page may be putting the last line in place.

PRAYER

Thank you for bringing the lines of my life together. Amen.

HOW TO EXPERIENCE
THE HOLY SPIRIT

*You shall receive power when the Holy Spirit has
come upon you.*

ACTS 1:8

How do we know grace has appeared in the form of
the Holy Spirit? Because we find ourselves doing
something we wouldn't normally be doing. "I was asked
if I would be willing to take on a particular service project," a Christian wrote, "and I knew. It wasn't even in an
area in which I felt competent, but I knew. This is it! This
is where God wants to work through me."

Who could possibly think that Jesus is the Messiah apart from the Holy Spirit? The Holy Spirit inspires us to think that thought. "No one can say 'Jesus is Lord'," Paul wrote, "except by the Holy Spirit" (1 Cor. 12:3).

Who could have the courage to share the deep places in their lives with other Christians apart from the Holy Spirit? The Holy Spirit gets us to feel that emotion. "Bearone another's burdens," Paul said, "and so fulfill the law of Christ" (Gal. 6:2).

Who could possibly find themselves giving of themselves in love to the uttermost, apart from the Spirit? A man shared with his church during worship how astounded he was at the amount of money he found himself giving away.

How do we know it's the Spirit? Because we aren't doing it. It is being done through us, not by us. We have been overpowered by a force other than our own pushing us to do it. "You shall receive power when the Holy Spirit has come upon you," Jesus promised.

How do we get the Spirit? We don't; the Spirit gets us. One way is through the church. "Since you are eager for manifestations of the Spirit," Paul wrote, "strive to excel in building up the church" (1 Cor. 14:12). We can't make it alone as Christians. The power just isn't there. All the above quotes are attributed to people in churches. The first church was galvanized by the Holy Spirit at Pentecost (Acts 2:1-4).

Even Jesus had to have other people with him. Yes, he

drew away to pray, and we need to as well. But there is something about the experience called "church" that can bring the Holy Spirit to us as nothing else can.

PRAYER

May I experience the Holy Spirit's power today. Amen.

HOW TO GET MORE OUT
OF LIFE

Lead...me to the rock that is higher than I.

PSALM 61:2

Why get up early on our day off, leave our eggs and three strips of bacon, corral the kids, get everyone into clean clothes, and go off to church?

Because we know we need something more. We get more breadth. "A new commandment I give to you," Jesus said, "that you love one another" (John 13:34). Going to church helps us love. We hear about people all over the world who need us. We also hear about brothers and sisters in Christ who need us. Some are right there beside us in the pew.

We get more depth. "Out of the depths I cry to thee, O Lord!" (Ps. 130:1). When we confess in church, we are plunged into the depths of who we are. That gives us more of ourselves. We just don't confess that often. With church, we can't avoid it. Church keeps us in touch with reality.

We get more height. "Lead...me to the rock that is higher than I," the psalmist wrote. We need something higher than we are to keep our egos in check. When we're on a mountain we see things differently. God was called "the Most High" (Dan. 3:26, Luke 1:32). The earliest name for God was El Shaddai, "the mountain one" (Gen. 49:25). Moses brought the tablets down from Mt. Sinai. Jesus was killed on Mt. Calvary.

After confessing our sin in church, we are taken by grace to the mountaintop with the declaration of pardon. Church reminds us that we are never left in our despair. We are never left in our sin. We may be plunged into the depths of whatever negative emotion or sin is troubling us, but in church we are raised out of it, at least for the moment, to the height of forgiveness.

That's why we find ourselves singing. We are overjoyed that we are not left in our sin and despair. We want to share our joy with others. And we find ourselves wanting to do something in the name of Christ for those who are hurting more than we are. All that is worth singing about, and we, who never sing during the week, find ourselves singing lustily in church. Me? Sing? Pure grace.

PRAYER

Thank you for the "more" I find at my church. Amen.

HOW TO SEE DOUBLE

*Demas, in love with this present world, has
deserted me.*

2 TIMOTHY 4:10

Paul had been abandoned by Demas, one of his most
trusted associates. The explanation given was that
Demas was "in love with this present world." Apparently, he loved this present world to the exclusion of the
divine world. He lacked perspective and the ability to
"see double"—to see both the present world and the divine world.

Our problem is that idols keep us stuck in this present
world. An idol is a god that obscures God. We may make

an idol of our jobs, for instance. We can't wait to get to work in the morning. Our work may be our fun. This is as it should be, of course. But often the divine world gets obscured.

We may make an idol of our families, in love with our spouses and "idolizing" our children. Again, this is as it should be—except that it is all too easy to attach ultimate meaning to them rather than proximate meaning. We live for them and forget living for God.

We may make an idol of our country. "My country right or wrong—but, right or wrong, my country." Our country is a great country, and we love it. But that does not mean that there are not many things about it that need correcting. Poverty is the Achilles' heel of capitalism, and we are not doing well by the millions of ill-clad, ill-fed, and ill-housed. Seeing through to God helps us see how to do better.

We may even idolize ourselves. The day begins and ends with us. We are at the center of our universe. It is difficult to see how there is anything more beyond. How can we see through to God when all we see is ourselves? It's not deliberate, but, in effect, we obscure God.

We need to develop double vision, seeing through this present world to include the world beyond. How do we do that? We don't. It's too much to ask. We're stuck with our idols. Seeing through and gaining perspective have to be accomplished for us. Whenever we see through, it is grace breaking through. It pushes our idols aside, at least for a while.

PRAYER

Help me see beyond this present world to your influence on it and through it. Amen.

HOW TO HANDLE DEATH

All these with one accord devoted themselves
to prayer.

ACTS 1:14

When someone we love dies, or when we think of our own dying, how do we handle it? Jesus had died, and his friends were hard-pressed to make sense of it.

There are those who say that the prospect of death can only turn us inward, that all we have is ourselves, which isn't much in the face of death. They argue that we must avoid the trite conventions of religion, which presuppose help in such matters. We must see reality for what it is—winter beyond summer, night beyond day, death beyond life. Our nobility is our ability to endure all weathers with equanimity.

There is a long and serious tradition behind this way of thinking. It is so deeply embedded in our history that it is in the Bible. "Vanity of vanities," says the writer of Ecclesiastes, "all is vanity and a striving after wind" (Eccles. 1:2, 14). All is vanity because all is annihilated by death. Consequently, it is vain to speculate on ultimate meaning, and it is vain to sugarcoat death.

There is, of course, another way to handle death. It was the way of the disciples after Jesus' death. "All these with one accord," the Bible says, "devoted themselves to prayer." Prayer is turning out rather than in. It is waiting for the sense to emerge from the nonsense. "Wait," Jesus told them, "for the promise of the Father" (Acts 1:4). That is how the meaning will break through the meaninglessness—by waiting.

Waiting is, of all things, the most difficult. We want action in a crisis. We want to do something, anything. "He charged them not to depart from Jerusalem, but to wait" (Acts 1:4). Departing was one thing they could have done. It wasn't safe to stay. So, when they found themselves going back to the upper room and devoting themselves to prayer, it could only be grace moving them to stay

The promise of the Father was the gift of the Holy Spirit, a gift of grace that comes with waiting, in prayer. "You shall receive power," Jesus tells them, "when the

Holy Spirit has come upon you" (Acts 1:8). It would come soon, at Pentecost, when the church would be born. The birth of the church would bring meaning out of the meaninglessness of Jesus' death.

The same can happen for us when a loved one dies. We find ourselves in prayer, waiting. When we wait, it is grace moving us to wait. Our own Pentecost will be soon. It is promised.

PRAYER

I pray for the patience to pray, while I wait for the gift of the Spirit. Amen.

HOW TO HANDLE DESPAIR

Let the day perish wherein I was born.

JOB 3:3

The low grade on the exam, the missed promotion on the job, the endless conflict at home—any of these events is enough to plunge you into despair. Job lost his health, his wealth, and his children. It was enough to prompt the despairing cry, "Let the day perish wherein I was born."

What happens in despair is that the self-reliance on which we prop our lives crumbles. But the crumbling is healthy. The Hebrew word for self-reliance, *batach*, means to be credulous, gullible. The ancient Hebrews used it negatively. Pinning your hope on yourself, they said, is characteristic of the fool.

"A fool is hotheaded and yet feels secure" (Prov. 14:16 NIV). But it is foolish to place our security in ourselves rather than in grace. Our despair is a gift redeeming us from self-reliance. It is a gift showing us we have placed our hope in a false sense of security.

Paul was in a desperate situation. The boat on which he was being taken to Rome was foundering. "This very night," he tells the crew, "there stood by me an angel of the God to whom I belong" (Acts 27:23). The angel of God comes to us in the night of our despair and says to us, "Do not be afraid" (Acts 27:24).

The graceful work of despair is the process the ancients called the "dark night of the soul." They realized that it was, paradoxically, through such "negative" experiences as despair that some of the most positive experiences of life could occur. God is coming to us through our least developed side, the side in which self-reliance does not work. No, this is not the only way God comes, but it is one way.

The gift of despair is that it will not allow us to stay where we are, where we are comfortable, secure, and undeveloped. That is why the Bible has such harsh things to say about idolatry. Idolatry is the attempt to create false security. It whispers that those areas of my life in which I am most comfortable—that is, most self-reliant—are the areas that are going to save me.

"When I am weak," Paul said, "then I am strong" (2 Cor. 12:10). When grace had made him no longer self-reliant, he could become God-reliant. "I have uttered what I did not understand," Job confesses to God, "Therefore I despise myself, and repent in dust and ashes" (Job 42:3, 6). Through the catalyst of his despair, God had arrived.

PRAYER

Please remind me that my despair is bringing me to you.
Amen.

HOW TO BE DISCIPLINED
IN FAITH

O LORD, *in the morning thou dost hear my voice.*

PSALM 5:3

A man gets up at 5:00 every morning and runs to a neighboring town and back. It is part of his daily routine. He is taking time for what he feels is important.

In a large metropolitan area, a businessperson arrives at the train station promptly at 7:05 every weekday morning, brings up the *Wall Street Journal* on an iPad, and has the necessary information by the time he or she arrives for work. It is part of the daily routine. Time is taken for what is deemed important.

A sophomore in high school spends every weekday from 7 to 10 p.m. on homework. It is part of her daily routine. She is taking time for what she feels is important.

The word *discipline* comes from the Latin word for "learn." "I am still learning" was Michelangelo's motto. He was highly disciplined, or he would not have been so productive.

For some reason, the word *discipline* has come into disrepute. But not for the psalmist. "O LORD, in the morning thou dost hear my voice." He took time for the first of three times a day Jews were to pray.

I stuffed my raincoat into the overhead bin and glanced over at what the man next to me was reading. I was astonished to see it was 2 Chronicles. "Well," I said, "that's pretty impressive reading you have there." He said it was for Sunday's Bible study at his church. He couldn't stop talking about his church.

One way to develop a discipline when it comes to matters of faith is to find ourselves doing what the psalmist did. He found himself praying every morning because of what was going on in his life. "Give heed to my groaning," he says to God (Ps. 5:1). "Hearken to the sound of my cry" (Ps. 5:2). He was at one of those points in life where his groans and cries were grace, moving him to pray.

Developing a discipline is not something we do out of the blue. It can only come out of the context of events. We don't develop a discipline so much as find ourselves disciplined. It is the circumstances of life that move us to pray. We don't move ourselves. Events become gifts; gifts become grace. Grace works through events.

We don't say, "I'm going to develop the discipline of prayer." That doesn't work. The discipline is soon dropped. Rather, we find ourselves praying. Why? Because grace, working through events, has moved us to pray. Our groans and cries have driven us not to despair but to our knees.

PRAYER

Thank you for your gift of grace when I most need it.
Amen.

HOW TO HANDLE
DISTANCE

My God, my God, why hast thou forsaken me?
MATTHEW 27:46

To one degree or another, we all feel distance. There is, for instance, the distance within ourselves. We feel distant from the person we want to be and hopeless to become the person God intended us to be. Even Jesus felt this distance as he battled with the devil during his temptations.

There is the distance between us and other people. We feel distant from others at work. We feel it from others around the world. Even in our own homes we can feel hopelessly distant from each other. Jesus felt such distance continually as he battled the scribes and Pharisees.

There is also the distance beyond us. "The silence of these infinite spaces frightens me," Blaise Pascal wrote. Try as we will, we are continually frustrated in overcoming the distance between us and God. Even Jesus felt this distance. "My God, my God," he cried from the cross, "why hast thou forsaken me?"

But often it is when we feel farthest that we are nearest. "When you think you are far from me, it is often then that I am the closest" (Thomas à Kempis in *The Imitation of Christ*). That suggests that we need not avoid our feelings of distance but rather feel them with what Kierkegaard called "passionate inwardness."

But where is the motivation to be passionately inward about our distances? Jesus is the motivation. He experienced every distance we experience. He experienced them passionately and triumphed accordingly. He beat back the devil. He won against the scribes and Pharisees. And he saw his last distance overcome in the Resurrection.

But where does the motivation come from to think about Jesus? From grace. Grace is what gets us to think about Jesus. When we think about Jesus, that is grace overcoming our distance. Why is it grace and not us? Because we do not willingly call up an image of Jesus. If we did, we wouldn't be feeling so hopeless and frustrated about the distance in our lives.

When we find ourselves imagining Jesus, we experience, at least for the moment, the joy of distance overcome.

PRAYER

When I feel distant from you and others and even from my self, help me see Jesus. Amen.

HOW TO HANDLE SHAME

The Lord turned and looked at Peter.

LUKE 22:61

The reason everyone likes Peter is that he denied Jesus just the way we all do. We all renege on our confessions of faith at one time or another. On being recognized as a follower of the arrested Jesus, Peter denied that he even knew him. It was so human.

It is the rhythm of the spiritual life to vacillate between affirmation and denial. Thomas Merton, the Trappist monk who captured the imagination of the world in the 1940s and 1950s, fills page after page wrestling with God.

It is no accident that the story of the Hebrew people includes a struggle for faith, as Jacob wrestles with the angel on the banks of the river Jabbok. His name is changed from Jacob to Israel, "he who strives with God" (footnote, Gen. 32:28).

Even Paul, who said that "if anyone is in Christ, there is a new creation" (2 Cor. 5:17 NRSV), vacillated between affirmation and denial. "I do not understand my own actions," he cries. "For I do not do what I want, but I do the very thing I hate" (Rom. 7:15). Presumably, as a follower of Christ, he would be doing what Christ wanted. But he finds himself acting against Christ at every turn.

Perhaps our denial began in college. Then we return to following Christ after the birth of our first child. At least we start going to church again. But the rhythm between affirmation and denial continues. On the one hand we believe; on the other, we don't. We are like the father of the boy with epilepsy. "I believe," he said to Jesus; "help my unbelief!" (Mark 9:24).

But all is not lost by our vacillating. Far from it. On Peter's third denial "the Lord turned and looked at Peter" (Luke 22:61). It must have cut him to the quick. Indeed, the Bible says "he went out and wept bitterly" (Luke 22:62). His tears were grace, beginning his transformation from coward to saint.

When the Lord turns and looks at us, everything changes. When we are as ashamed of letting Jesus down as

Peter was, then it is possible we, too, will see him looking at us. Our tears will be grace, beginning our transformation.

PRAYER

Whenever I deny Jesus, may I see him looking at me as he looked at Peter. Amen.

HOW TO FEEL GOOD
ABOUT YOURSELF

Abraham...went out, not knowing where he
was to go.

HEBREWS 11:8

It's interesting how seldom motivation is discussed in the Bible.

"The LORD said to Abram, 'Go...to the land that I will show you'" (Gen. 12:1). And "Abraham...went out, not knowing where he was to go." The word heard was the word obeyed. Indeed, "to hear" in the Hebrew means "to obey."

Jesus rarely discussed motivation. He spoke directly: Turn the other cheek. Go the second mile. Love your neighbor. Judge not. Follow me.

After his release from Iran in 1982, one of the American embassy hostages told of coming home and finding himself in the West Point Chapel. His voice broke as he told what he saw printed on the wall: "Duty. Honor. Country." He told how those three words had put his life back together—and how they had served to carry him and the others through their 444-day ordeal.

God first—the chapel. Then duty—obeying the ethical commands of the Bible. Then honor—we feel honorable as we do our duty. Then country—serving others. "What does the LORD require of you?" (Mic. 6:8).

First the theology, then the sociology, then the psychology. We hear the divine command; that's the theology. "Do justice" (Mic. 6:8). We find ourselves obeying it in society; that's the sociology. We feel good about our obedience; that's the psychology. And it does good as well as feels good; we find ourselves serving others.

The psychology is the by-product of the theology and sociology. We feel good about ourselves because we have obeyed God and served others.

This is the reverse of our usual attempts to find happiness in which happiness is the goal instead of God. The wisdom of the Bible is that happiness finds us when we find ourselves obeying God's command to serve. When we find ourselves serving, it is grace moving us to serve. Why grace? Because we won't serve voluntarily. How do we know? Because we haven't served. We feel that our lives are good enough without adding a soup kitchen.

Service is why the incarnation of God's command, Jesus, was called the Suffering Servant. And it is why the Suffering Servant said, "[I] came not to be served but to serve" (Mark 10:45).

We can stand around arguing forever about whether we should love our neighbors. Do it, the Bible says, then we will know it. We will know the divine command was right once we find ourselves moved by grace to obey it.

Abraham went out not knowing where he was to go. But he got there.

PRAYER

I need your help to do what you would have me do.
Amen.

HOW TO BE ENCOURAGED
IN FAITH

Barnabas took him, and brought him to the apostles.

ACTS 9:27

Following his conversion, Paul hurried to Damascus to link up with the disciples. They were naturally afraid of him because of his history of persecution. Barnabas was the first to befriend him and helped him gain entry to the group. "Barnabas took him, and brought him to the apostles."

Barnabas, whose name meant "Son of encourage-ment," was giving Paul the courage he needed to obey his call. He was willing to stand by Paul in his ostracism. In a word, he was being the church for Paul.

The church is composed of the people who stand by us in our loneliness. For every Paul there is a Barnabas, someone sent by grace to encourage us on our journey of faith. Subsequently, Paul and Barnabas traveled all over the Mediterranean world together.

Who first encouraged us in our faith? A parent, teacher, friend, husband, wife? There could be no faith without a Barnabas at some time or other. Virtually everyone comes to Christ through someone else. Even Paul came to Christ through the very Christians he had persecuted.

Our call is to be a Barnabas for others. Who could we "take and bring to the disciples"? A parent, teacher, friend, husband, wife? Many Christians are afraid to be sons and daughters of encouragement.

But if someone has come to us as our Barnabas, courage can replace fear. All we need is the image of that person to move us to become a Barnabas for someone else.

For me, the image is of a seminary student down the street from my college. Somehow he came across my roommate and a few others. It was sheer happenstance, sheer grace. They began meeting as a small group of disciples.

The image is also of my roommate. He invited me to

the next meeting, and we met weekly thereafter for prayer and sharing and reading the Bible. The group became my closest friends in college, and most of us ended up in the same fraternity together.

But I would not have had such a close relationship to Christ if that seminary student had not been a Barnabas to my roommate and if my roommate had not been a Barnabas to me. He "took me, and brought me to the apostles."

PRAYER

Thank you for sending me a Barnabas whenever I have needed one. Amen.

HOW TO HANDLE AN
ENEMY

Love your enemies.

MATTHEW 5:44

There were three forms of love in the culture of Jesus' time. One was passionate—*eros*, from which we get our word *erotic*. Eros was the god of sexual love. The Romans called him Cupid. The word *eros* was also used for ambition, which, like sex, could be either positive or negative. Passion can easily use other people for its own ends. Surprisingly, the word *eros* is never used in the New Testament.

Another form of love was reciprocal—*philia*, from

which we get our word *Philadelphia*, the city of brotherly love. *Philia* was love of those who love us, such as love of friends and relatives. The passion of *eros* was gone. But *philia* was warm if not hot. It meant friendship, companionship. It even meant the way the disciples loved Jesus (John 16:27).

But *philia*, as *eros*, had its Achilles' heel. "If you love those who love you," Jesus asked, "what reward have you? ... What more are you doing than others?" (Matt. 5:46-47). Consequently, *philia* makes the grade only twenty-six times in the New Testament, an average of only once per book. There was a third form of love—*agape* (uh-GAH-pay), enemy love. It was the distinctly Christian form of love and is used 314 times in the New Testament. The word was there in the Greek, all right, but with a different meaning and rarely used. It meant no more than to be satisfied with something, and it was so rare that only one example of it as a noun has ever been found in pre-Christian Greek.

Eros was passionate; *agape* compassionate. *Eros* was I-centered; *agape* you-centered. *Eros* was ambitious; *agape* was ambitious for others. *Philia* was love of those who love us; *agape* was love of even those who do not love us. *Philia* was love of our friends; *agape* was love of our enemies. *Philia* could even be love of Christ; *agape* was putting love of Christ into action—with the poor, the sick, the hungry (Matt. 25:35).

When we find ourselves centered outside ourselves, it has to be grace; it can't be us, because we are too centered in *eros* and *philia*. Grace is what brings us over into *agape*. When we find ourselves loving our enemy at work, it has to be grace; it can't be us, because we wouldn't do it. How do we know we wouldn't do it? Because we haven't done it! It's too much for us. Therefore, when we find ourselves loving an enemy, we know it's a power greater than our own. We call that power grace.

PRAYER

When I find myself loving beyond what I am capable of, help me recognize that it is your pure grace. Amen.

HOW TO HANDLE GUILT

Saul increased all the more in strength.

ACTS 9:22

Guilt opens up an area of life over which we are powerless. Therefore, it becomes a bridge over which we are moved from can-do to can't-do.

When we are in our can-do way of life, we don't need God. But when we are thrown into our can't-do way of life, only God will suffice.

To be sure, we can work hard at getting rid of our guilt. We can read the self-help books. We can talk to a therapist. We can pray. We can apologize. We can try to do all the right things.

"You, therefore, must be perfect," Jesus said (Matt. 5:48). But he said it because he knew we couldn't be perfect. We can't do all the right things. If we were even to approach perfection, it would have to be grace doing the approaching through us. God can arrive across the bridge of guilt.

How do we know it's grace? We leave the past with its guilt and are freed to live now, at least for the moment. Because we find ourselves living more in the present; we are spontaneous and full of energy.

"Since all have sinned and fall short of the glory of God," Paul wrote, "they are justified by his grace as a gift, through the redemption which is in Christ Jesus" (Rom. 3:23-24). It wasn't until Paul met Jesus on the Road to Damascus that he was freed from his guilt over persecuting Christians. His freedom was pure grace.

How do we meet Jesus? Historically, through other people. "I see the Christ in the other," it is said. Grace sent Ananias to Paul to explain what had happened on the Road to Damascus. Ananias had not wanted to go (Acts 9:13). Therefore, it had to be grace; it couldn't be Ananias.

From then on, Paul's spontaneity knew no bounds, and he "increased all the more in strength." He had been freed from his guilt by the grace of Christ and of Ananias. Who has God used to help free us?

PRAYER

Thank you for using my guilt to bring me closer
to you. Amen.

HOW TO BE PERSISTENT
IN FAITH

*When the Son of man comes, will he find faith
on earth?*

LUKE 18:8

One can feel Jesus' anguish as he asks this question.
He has just told a story about faith, only to find
himself wondering if the faithful will remain so.

How do we persist in the faith? Jesus told a story
about a widow who kept "bothering" a judge to get him
to hear her case (Luke 18:1-5). She persisted until she
won. "Will not God vindicate his elect," Jesus asks, "who

cry to him day and night?" (Luke 18:7) Grace moves us to cry out.

The Jews of Jesus' time were expected to pray at least three times a day—9 A.M., noon, and 3:00 P.M. Most of us are lucky to get in one prayer a day, let alone three. Muslims pray five times a day.

Perhaps the key to praying more often is to identify with the widow. She was one of society's helpless. The corrupt judges of the day would respond to influence and money but not to poverty. God is not a corrupt judge, but if grace can give us the image of one in dire need, it may help us persist in the faith.

The trouble is that we are more often like the corrupt judge. We, too, are more responsive to money and influence than to images of widows in dire need.

There are times, of course, when we are in dire need—when a loved one dies, when we are told we have a serious illness, when things become intolerable at work. Then we approach God with great persistence. But how can we imagine ourselves in dire need constantly, day and night?

Most of us probably never will, hence Jesus' anguished question. We all need grace. Under the pressure of life's events, grace happens, and we see the image of the persistent widow before the reluctant judge. We carry it with us during the day and into sleep at night. It is pure grace that such an image should persist in our consciousness, let alone in our unconsciousness. Perhaps the imagination, the giver and receiver of images, is the "image of God" in us (Gen. 1:26).

PRAYER

May the stories Jesus told become the ones I think about, day and night. Amen.

HOW TO HANDLE FEAR

Do not be afraid, Mary.

LUKE 1:30

The angel who came to announce God so frightened Mary that he said to her, "Do not be afraid, Mary." The shepherds were also afraid (Luke 2:10). So was Zechariah (Luke 1:13). Paul was afraid (Acts 18:9). The disciples were afraid when Jesus stilled the storm (Mark 4:41), when he cured a demoniac (Mark 5:15), when he healed a woman (Mark 5:33), and when he was transfigured (Mark 9:6). The Gospel of Mark even ends on the word *afraid* (Mark 16:8).

The curious thing is that each of these experiences of fear is coupled with an experience of God. It has been said that there are only two basic emotions: love and fear. God appears in both. The Bible says "God is love" (1 John 4:16). It doesn't say "God is fear," but it clearly suggests that, when we are afraid, we can experience God.

Some may object that this is simply "foxhole faith" and that as soon as we leave the foxhole, we will leave the faith. But there is more to fear than that. There is nothing wrong with foxhole faith. If God can't be in the foxholes of life, then what kind of God have we?

It is good to pay attention to our fears. They are not only humbling us but also bringing us God—if, that is, we find ourselves staying with them long enough for God to arrive. The ability to stay can only be grace. Left to our own devices we wouldn't stay with them. We'd run from them into activity. How do we know? It's what we do!

PRAYER

Help me realize you are coming to me in my fear. Amen.

HOW TO HANDLE
IDOLATRY

I see four men.

DANIEL 3:25

How do we hold fast to God? There are so many lesser gods that masquerade as God, each one clamoring for allegiance. We call such lesser gods idols. An idol is a god that would be God.

Nebuchadnezzar, king of Babylon in 585 B.C., set up an idol. It measured six by sixty cubits (Dan. 3:1). A cubit was the length of an arm from the elbow to the tip of the middle finger, about eighteen inches. Six by sixty would make an idol 9 feet wide by 90 feet tall. Everyone was to "fall down and worship" at the foot of the idol (Dan. 3:5).

Three young men decided they wouldn't do that. So the king had a furnace heated and threw them in. In a stunning image, the Bible reminds us of the presence of God in even the most trying circumstances. The king gets down on his hands and knees to see how the fire is progressing. "I see four men," he cries, "and the appearance of the fourth is like a son of the gods" (Dan. 3:24-25).

How were Shadrach, Meshach, and Abednego—captured Jews in an alien land—able to hold fast to God? They were in the habit of doing so. It's as simple as that. They kept the dietary laws (Dan. 1:8-16). They prayed three times a day (Dan. 6:10). And they had a personified grace in there with them.

It wasn't only that they were more courageous than anyone else. It's that they had better habits. They simply did what they had always been doing, and, when the chips were down, their habits stood them in good stead. Hemingway defined courage as "grace under pressure." It might also be defined as "habits under pressure."

Where are such habits learned but in families? They were young men, fresh from their families. Grace had given the ancient Jews their habits, such as these about the dietary laws and praying three times a day. Moses contributed to habits with ten (Exod. 20:3-17). Jesus distilled them to two (Matt. 22:38).

When we find ourselves teaching such habits in our homes, grace is again at work. How so? It is moving us to do the teaching. Prayer at bedtimes is grace. "Grace" is said at meals. Bible stories like this one are read. Normally, we are unmotivated to read the Bible aloud or pray with our kids. Therefore, it has to be grace; it can't be us. Grace is doing the teaching through us.

PRAYER

Help me remember the habits of staying close to you. Amen.

HOW TO KEEP GOD
ACCESSIBLE

Our God is a consuming fire.
HEBREWS 12:29

Often God seems remote and sometimes even inaccessible. We need help in reaching God. We may even feel that God has left us in our hour of need.

Our help in reaching God comes from Jesus. Jesus mediates the power of God. Jesus is like the magnifying glass through which the sun shines onto paper, like the experiment we did when we were children. Jesus is between us and God, focusing the energy of God on the fragile paper of our lives and setting us on fire. "Our God," the Bible says, "is a consuming fire."

Fire is an age-old symbol of regeneration, of cleaning the slate, starting over, getting going again. It was fire at the burning bush, fire at Pentecost, fire in the halos of the saints, fire in the candles of the churches. Whenever we dream of fire, it can be a dream of new life. "If anyone is in Christ," Paul wrote, "there is a new creation" (2 Cor. 5:17 NRSV).

The word Paul used to explain the magnifying power of Jesus was *dunamis,* from which we get our word *dynamic.* "The gospel," he wrote, "is the power of God for salvation" (Rom. 1:16). As the energy of God flows through the example of Jesus, we are set on fire, empowered to do the things Jesus did. In a remarkable assertion, Jesus said, "The one who believes in me will also do the works that I do and, in fact, will do greater works than these, because I am going to the Father" (John 14:12 NRSV).

The reason we are able to do these greater works is that grace has given us the gift of the Holy Spirit. "I will ask the Father," Jesus said, "and he will give you another Advocate, to be with you forever" (John 14:16 NRSV). The Holy Spirit empowers Jesus as magnifier, concentrating the rays of God on the events of our lives. The concentration is of such power that even the ugliest events can be transformed.

PRAYER

*Thank you for the dynamic power of your Holy Spirit,
regenerating my life. Amen.*

HOW TO PUT GOD FIRST

Seek first his kingdom.

MATTHEW 6:33

Sin is putting ourselves first. Salvation is putting God first. How do we get from the one to the other? We have to be brought. What brings us? Anything that knocks us out of first place. It could be falling in love. It could be failing at work. It could be anything.

How do we get from loving or failing to Jesus, since he is the one who saves us? Loving and failing bring us. When we are first, we don't need Jesus. We can never hear him say, "Seek first his kingdom." But when we are taken out of ourselves by love or failure or whatever, then we can hear him. Then he can save us.

Sin is self-reliance at the expense of other- and God-reliance. The only way we will be taken out of first place is by being taken beyond ourselves by some positive or negative event or series of events.

We often do something because it is good for us, when we should be doing it because it is also good for others. We fail to see that self-fulfillment is a by-product of self-giving. And we will never see that it is until the positive and negative events of life have added up sufficiently to move us to see.

And what if events don't add up? What if we remain self-centered? Then we remain self-centered. The exhortations of family, friends, and Bible are of no avail until we have lived enough to hear them.

But eventually life's events can add up. One day a word or event will be the final weight placed on the scales of our life, and we will hear Jesus say, "Seek first his kingdom."

Later, looking back, we may be surprised to hear ourselves saying that such a word or event was grace. Later still, we may be equally surprised to hear ourselves saying that the whole series of words and events leading up to that word or event was grace.

PRAYER

Help me realize that whatever knocks me out of first place could be bringing me to you. Amen.

HOW TO FOLLOW JESUS

Follow me.

MATTHEW 4:19

The first thing Peter and Andrew did was follow Jesus. No questions asked. "He said to them, 'Follow me' ...Immediately they left their nets and followed him" (Matt. 4:19-20). Suddenly, Jesus had dropped into their lives. "As he walked by the Sea of Galilee, he saw two brothers" (Matt. 4:18). All happenstance. All grace.

We come to Jesus full of enthusiasm. No questions asked. Often we are very young. We come because it is the thing to do. It is a rite of passage. It is something our parents want. It may be something we want. In any case, there is rarely any questioning. We simply follow as we are told and, often, with enthusiasm. All happenstance from our birth. All grace.

Or we come to Jesus later in life because, again, it is the thing to do, because a friend has suggested it, because we want the children to go to Sunday school, because it would please our spouse, or simply because we want to. In any event, we tend to follow and, often, with enthusiasm. Again, all grace.

I think of following my guide up the Matterhorn in Switzerland. We arose at 3:30 A.M. in the hut at the base of the mountain. We got up early to beat the avalanches that come with the afternoon sun. My guide led the way unerringly. I followed with no questions asked and with great enthusiasm. By 7:30 we were on top.

Peter followed his leader all the way. Indeed, it is Peter who makes the great confession of faith at Caesarea Philippi. "Who do you say that I am?" Jesus asks (Matt. 16:15). "You are the Christ," Peter replies, "the Son of the living God" (Matt. 16:16). The revelation came after the years of following.

We may not know who Jesus is at first. We follow him as dutiful confirmands or grudging spouses. But later it comes to us that we have been following one who is the Christ, the Son of the living God, the Lord of life.

PRAYER

Help me recognize you anew today as the Lord of my life.
Amen.

HOW TO FORGIVE

How often should I forgive?
MATTHEW 18:21 NRSV

On their way to Jerusalem, Peter asked Jesus how many times he should forgive someone. Seven?

Jesus said, No, "seventy times seven" (Matt. 18:22). Then he told a story to prove his point.

The vice president in charge of loans at First National Bank loaned a man ten million dollars for his company. The time came to pay it back, the man couldn't, so the loan officer started foreclosure proceedings. But the man pleaded with him to extend the note six more months, saying that he'd have the money by that time. The loan officer had mercy on him and agreed to give him the extra time.

Then this same man, on his way out of the bank, bumped into a man on the street who owed him two dollars. He grabbed the debtor by the throat and demanded that he pay; the poor fellow said he'd have it by Sunday, but the man called the police and had the debtor thrown in jail. When the loan officer heard about it, he sent the sheriff after the ten-million-dollar man and had him jailed as well. Only Jesus ups the ante. He says the loan officer "handed him over to be tortured until he would pay his entire debt" (Matt. 18:34 NRSV).

Our job as Christians is to forgive. Forgiving is at the heart of the gospel. It is unconditional love in action. The word for "forgive" in both the Hebrew and Greek means "let go." We are to let go of what the other person has done to us. Only, it isn't we who are letting go; it is grace through us. Left to our own devices, we would never let go. We are too angry. But we are not left to our own devices. That is the good news of the gospel.

If we do not forgive, we, too, are in jail, imprisoned by what we will not let go. The memory of what the other person did to us is torturing us. It bothers our eating and sleeping. It ruins our relationship with the person and leaks out into our other relationships.

Some of Jesus' toughest language was reserved for those

who would not forgive. Regarding the torturing of the unforgiving debtor, Jesus said: "So also my heavenly Father will do to every one of you, if you do not forgive…from your heart" (Matt. 18:35). And in the Sermon on the Mount he made it clear that "if you do not forgive others, neither will your Father forgive your trespasses" (Matt. 6:15 NRSV).

When we find ourselves forgiving, it is grace giving us the courage to forgive. We could never do it on our own. How do we know? We never have!

PRAYER

Thank you for your grace that gives me the power to forgive.
Amen.

HOW TO BE MOTIVATED
TO FORGIVE

Lord, do not hold this sin against them.

ACTS 7:60

It's one thing to know we should forgive. It's another to know how to do it. One motivation for forgiving is having been forgiven ourselves. Few experiences give us a more vivid awareness of grace than being forgiven. We don't deserve to be forgiven; we deserve to be punished. Yet here we are being forgiven. It has to be pure grace.

Paul had such an experience. He held the sport coats for a mob while they dropped rocks on a man's head.

126

Then he heard the man say, "Lord, do not hold this sin against them." It had to be grace. Stephen was doing for Paul what Jesus had done on the cross. "Father, forgive them," Jesus had said, "for they know not what they do" (Luke 23:34).

Most of us need to see faith in action before we will be moved to forgive. We need a mentor in the faith. We need to see someone being Jesus for us, incarnating forgiveness. It could happen as early as childhood. As we remember how our parents forgave us time and again, it can motivate us to forgive.

I remember driving on a highway in Nebraska. I had just gotten my license and was taking over from my father for a spell as we headed east from vacation. As the light changed, the person in front of me suddenly stopped, and I, following too closely, ran into her. "Oh, Bobby, Bobby," my father said. That was all. Nothing about the inconvenience of finding a garage to fix the front end. Nothing about hassling with the insurance company. Nothing about having to find a place to stay that night while we waited for the car to be fixed. It was pure forgiveness and has stuck with me ever since.

Stephen's incredible act must have burned itself into Paul. It must have been one factor, if not the major one, in bringing him to Christ. One man's forgiveness as he lay dying brought Paul to Christ's forgiveness. It enabled Paul to forgive as he had been forgiven.

The one who forgives us is playing the role of Christ for us.

PRAYER

Whenever I have trouble forgiving, help me remember Stephen. Amen.

HOW TO FORGIVE
BEFORE IT'S TOO LATE

As the Lord has forgiven you, so you also must forgive.

COLOSSIANS 3:13

The story is told of a man who looked up from his hospital bed in cardiac care, tears filling his eyes.

"Would you call my daughter?" he asked the nurse. "I live alone, and she is the only family I have." His breathing suddenly sped up, as if he were about to have another heart attack.

"Nurse," he asked, "could you get me a pencil and

paper?" She dug a scrap of yellow paper and a pen from her pocket and set them on his bedside table. Then she called his daughter.

"You must not let him die," his daughter said. "Dad and I had a terrible argument a year ago. I haven't seen him since. All these months I've wanted to go ask him for forgiveness."

The nurse returned to her patient. He lay unmoving. His pulse was gone. She looked at the heart monitor. Not a beat. The whole medical team worked on him, but there was no response.

His daughter arrived. The nurse led her into the nurses' lounge and told her the news. "I loved him," his daughter said. "I want to see him." She went to his bed and buried her face in the sheets.

The nurse backed away. As she did, her hand fell on a scrap of yellow paper. She picked it up. It read: "My dearest Janie, I forgive you. I pray you will also forgive me. I know that you love me. I love you, too. Daddy."

PRAYER

Help me go to anyone I haven't yet forgiven. Amen.

HOW TO LOVE FREELY

*Just as I have loved you, you also should love
one another.*

JOHN 13:34 NRSV

The best gift we can give is to love without strings. It is to love other people just as they are.

"I know we've been going through a lot," a man said to his wife. "I know our lifestyles are different. But I just wanted to tell you I support you in what you feel you have to do to be you." He was loving her freely, without reservation, just as she was.

It was the presence of Christ in my friend's life that was freeing him to free his wife. Because God loved him freely in the gift of Christ, he could love her freely, too.

Remarkably, when we love another freely, we find that it frees the other to love us freely in return. That does not always happen, of course, and loving freely makes us vulnerable. The father of the prodigal son must have been hurting as he watched his son leave the family farm. God was hurting as Jesus was dying.

It is when we are loved freely, as God loves us freely, that we are given the power to be the persons we were meant to be. Our parents, our children, our friends, our spouses, when they are loving us freely, they are loving us as God is loving us. Then, when we fail, it is we who fail. "I have sinned," the prodigal son said. He could not say, "You caused me to sin by letting me go."

Of course, when we love freely, the other person may not freely love us back. The other person may even use us. That is the risk we take in loving freely. That is why Jesus was thought of as Isaiah's Suffering Servant (Isa. 53). Love suffers, or it is not love.

But surely the risk of loving freely is a better risk to take than loving with strings. Because when I love you with an agenda, I am not freeing you to be you. Loving you freely means I am giving up my need to run your life, which is the very thing that frees you to run your own life most effectively.

When we love freely, it has to be grace. It can't be us,

because we don't love freely, not without help. That help is grace.

PRAYER

Help me love freely, no strings attached. Amen.

HOW TO HANDLE
FRUSTRATION

Strive first for the kingdom of God.
MATTHEW 6:33 NRSV

We are so easily frustrated by the little things of life—losing the car keys, being late for an appointment, forgetting to turn off the coffee. That's why we need the big things to put the little things in perspective. "Strive first for the kingdom of God," Jesus said, "and all these things will be given to you as well"—food, drink, clothes, health.

Big-picture people can handle the little frustrations,

whereas little-picture people get done in by them. "The great use of life," William James said, "is to spend it for what outlasts it." That's the kind of big-picture idea that can put losing the car keys in perspective. What are we spending our lives on? Will it outlast us?

Holocaust survivor Viktor Frankl, while in a Nazi concentration camp, discovered that the people who survived were often those who were attached to something bigger than they were—anything from love of their families to helping other inmates.

There are no calls in the Bible to little things, only to big things. "Lead my people out of Egypt." "Form a new nation." "Seek justice." "Help the widow and the orphan." "Take up your cross." "Follow me." "I was not disobedient to the heavenly vision," Paul said (Acts 26:19). He could say that because with the call came the ability to obey it. "To this day," he said, "I have had the help that comes from God" (Acts 26:22).

Sometimes we don't have enough faith that we will get this kind of help. We can read the Bible and hear the call, but we fail to obey the call because of our timidity. We get caught up in the little things, as Martha, when only "one thing is needful," as Jesus says (Luke 10:42). Preparing her meal at that point was not as important as listening to him.

Keeping our eyes fixed on the big things of life requires discernment. Reading Bible stories about calls is clearly "the help that comes from God," namely, grace. How do we know it's grace? Because without grace's help, we wouldn't be reading the Bible.

Such stories show us how big-picture people can handle the little things of life. As the philosopher Nietzsche once observed, "Those who have a Why to live can bear with almost any How."

PRAYER

Help me "strive first for the kingdom" and have a big-picture view. Amen.

HOW TO RELY ON GOD

The Lord will fight for you, and you have only to be still.

EXODUS 14:14

The Israelites could not have been in a worse situation. If they went forward in the Exodus, they might never reach the Promised Land. If they returned to Egypt, they might be worked to death. All Moses told them to do was to rely on God. "The Lord will fight for you," he said, "and you have only to be still."

The premise is that, when we have a tough emotional problem, it could be God on the way. Like any premise, this one takes faith. The faith is that there is a God who stands by us in our suffering. More precisely, it is the faith that God arrives in our suffering, that our suffering brings God to us.

How can this be? The Judeo-Christian God, for the first time in history, was a suffering God. The God of Abraham, Sarah, Ruth, and Jesus is a God who suffers when we suffer. "My heart recoils within me," Hosea writes for God, "my compassion grows warm and tender" (Hos. 11:8). "For God so loved the world that he gave his only Son" (John 3:16), who was to suffer on a cross.

Having this kind of God changes how we look at our emotional problems. It means we are not alone in dealing with them. "For we have not a high priest who is unable to sympathize with our weaknesses" (Heb. 4:15). We have a God in the form of Jesus, "who in every respect has been tested as we are" (Heb. 4:15 NRSV).

Next time we have an emotional problem, the God who suffers with us may bring to mind Moses, who had his own share of emotional problems leading the Israelites. Grace will remind us how Moses told the suffering people, "The LORD will fight for you, and you have only to be still." Grace alone can keep us still.

PRAYER

Help me remember that my problem can be bringing me to you. Amen.

HOW TO USE OUR GIFT

Having gifts that differ... let us use them.

ROMANS 12:6

The word *gift*, we remember, has the same root as the word *grace* in the New Testament. Grace enters our life at the point of our gift.

The New Testament word for "gift" also has the same root as the word *charisma*. When we use our gift we become charismatic. People are drawn to us. We laugh easily. We feel good about ourselves. It shows.

But how do we know what our gift is? Perhaps a single word says it best. We know we're living out of our gift when we experience joy. The New Testament word for "gift" also has the same root as the word for "joy." The Gospels begin and end on notes of joy. It is joy that the wise men feel at the birth of Jesus (Matt. 2:10). And it is joy that the disciples feel at the return of Jesus after his death. "They returned to Jerusalem with great joy" (Luke 24:52).

The reason for the joy was the gift of Jesus. Our gift is not just what we do that makes us laugh easily and feel good about ourselves. Our gift is Jesus, and our particular charisma as Christians is that we are attracting people to him. People are drawn to us not only because we are living out of our gift but also because we are living out of the gift of Jesus. It is perhaps because of this gift of Jesus, even more than our personal gift, that we laugh easily and feel good about ourselves.

Curiously, the New Testament word for *gift* also has the same root as the word *eucharist*. In the eucharist we give thanks with joy for the gift of Jesus. And it is this gift that makes our personal gift especially charismatic.

Peter was in the right business. It was his gift to run a fishing company, but he did not really get going in his business until his greater gift, the gift of Jesus, was given to him. Remarkably, there is not a single instance in the Gospels of Peter's catching a fish without the help of Jesus.

PRAYER

Help me identify my gift and use it for Christ. Amen.

HOW TO VIEW LIFE
AS A GIFT

God will provide.

GENESIS 22:8

How do we view life as a gift—the bad things as well as the good? It can only be grace when we view calamity as a gift or when we remember to be thankful for a success. Abraham, for instance, was constantly building altars on his travels to commemorate the presence of God in his life (Gen. 12:7-8; 13:18).

Every call in the Bible comes in a profoundly disruptive experience. Moses, disrupted in a happy but inconsequential

141

life as a shepherd. Gideon, disrupted in his farming business. Hosea, in an unhappy marriage. Isaiah, in exile. Hannah, unable to conceive.

The crises of life can make us more available to God than ever. They can be viewed as God's attempt to identify people of faith. "Now I know," God says, after Abraham passes the test of faith (Gen. 22:12). God doesn't really know how faithful we are until our faith has been tested in a crisis.

Grace also helps us remember that God will provide. On the one hand, Abraham is tested; on the other hand, grace shows him there will be a way out. "God will provide," Abraham says as he prepares to burn his son as a sacrifice. And God does provide. Abraham sees a ram caught in a thicket and substitutes it for his son. Promptly he names the place, "The LORD will provide" (Gen. 22:14).

God will provide for those whom God tests in tough times. But we wouldn't know that if grace hadn't told us.

PRAYER

Help me remember that life is a gift bringing me to you.
Amen.

HOW TO USE OUR
SPIRITUAL GIFT

There are varieties of gifts
1 CORINTHIANS 12:4

One of the extraordinary things about the first church was the incredible variety of spiritual gifts. Paul listed gifts of wisdom, knowledge, faith, healing, miracles, prophecy, and tongues (1 Cor. 12:8). The list could be virtually endless. Grace lavishes the church with these gifts of the Spirit.

Our spiritual gift is just that, a gift. It is given to us, and we have very little to do with it. "There are varieties of gifts," Paul told the church, "but the same Spirit." Our gift is a gift of the Spirit.

The word the early Christians used for gifts was *charismata,* and everyone in a church was charismatic. It isn't just so-called dynamic leaders who are charismatic. Everyone is charismatic because everyone is spiritually gifted. Everyone is "inspired," a word coming from the root for "spirit within."

The church members are the people who help evoke our gifts. "Hey," they say, "you've got this incredible gift of..." We know it's our gift when we're not self-conscious. We know it when we're having fun. We can't have fun and be self-conscious.

"Do not neglect the gift you have," Timothy is told (1 Tim. 4:14). The church members not only help us identify and use our spiritual gift but also won't let us get away with not using it. "Practice these duties," Timothy is told, "devote yourself to them, so that all may see your progress" (1 Tim. 4:15).

Who were the ones primarily to see his progress? The church. "To each is given the manifestation of the Spirit," Paul explains, "for the common good" (1 Cor. 12:7). We are to use our gift for the common good of the church. It is for the inspiration of all.

Paul sees this use of our gift in the life of the church as the way the Spirit increases in the church. "Since you are eager for manifestations of the Spirit," he writes, "strive to excel in building up the church" (1 Cor. 14:12).

If we want to be inspired, Paul is saying, all we have to do is exercise our spiritual gift in the life of our church. It is an immensely practical answer to the perennial question, "How can I experience God?"

PRAYER

Help me discover and use my spiritual gift. Amen.

HOW TO FIND GOD IN
SUFFERING

I have been crucified with Christ.
GALATIANS 2:20

The remarkable thing about a suffering God is that
God is no longer aloof. For Christians, God has become one of us in the form of Jesus; and when Jesus hangs
on the cross, the image presented to the world is of a God
who is so involved with humanity that God is willing to
suffer.

Because God suffers with us, we suffer with others
in their "crucifixions." It troubles us, for instance, when

people we know are sick or in distress. We find ourselves going to them in hospitals and jails. Our going is grace, not ourselves.

Because of the suffering God, we find ourselves also reaching out to people we don't even know, serving in the local homeless shelter, tutoring a struggling student. We are incarnating Christian love, *agape*. Christians all over the world find themselves in hospitals, leprosaria, and food dispensaries where they are healing the sick, working for social justice, and reaching out to the poor and oppressed.

As Christians we also find ourselves identifying with Jesus in our own suffering. "I have been crucified with Christ," Paul wrote. "It is no longer I who live, but Christ who lives in me." It is this identification with Jesus that gives the Christian such a remarkable grounding in hope—hope for a better world, hope that suffering can be overcome, hope that the political, social, and economic causes of suffering will be addressed as forthrightly as the physical.

It is this feeling of being one with Jesus that gave the first Christians the hope that their suffering was accomplishing something, that it was for the good of the world, that it was making a difference. Paul became a prisoner in Rome. He could be executed at any time. But grace was using his suffering to transform reality because it was suffering done in the context of a God who loves so much that that God suffers with us, as proved in the suffering on the cross.

PRAYER

May I find myself reaching out more for Christ, finding him in the suffering. Amen.

HOW TO FIND GOD IN JUSTICE

I was hungry and you gave me food.

MATTHEW 25:35

One way we know it's grace is when we find ourselves doing something we wouldn't normally do for social justice.

A United Nations survey shows that America is slipping toward a category of countries like Guatemala and Brazil in which economic stratification is most pronounced, where the national per capita income is four times or more higher than the average income of the poor.

Grace is what moves us to reach out to the poor, the sick, the outcast. Grace is what beats our narcissism occasionally and turns it into altruism. How do we know it's grace? Because without grace, we remained stuck in our narcissism.

It may be a family problem or a business problem or a health problem or a financial problem that holds us back. Whatever it is, try as we will, we cannot seem to free ourselves of it in order to go forward with life, more life, life that includes people less fortunate than we are.

Or it may be that we are problem-free and are held back simply by life's being so good in this dimension that we have no need of another. None of our kids is on drugs. We're doing well at work. Our health is fine, and our finances secure. We don't have to be saved from anything. In such circumstances, of course, our sin is that we know no sin.

"I was hungry and you gave me food," Jesus said. When we find ourselves doing something for a more equitable society, that is grace. Grace has moved us to act.

PRAYER

I need you to keep me aware of others less fortunate than I. Do not let me look at the world with dry eyes. Amen.

HOW TO DO GOOD

He has showed you ... what is good.

MICAH 6:8

We know the good, Micah says, because God has showed it to us. When Micah says "good," he is not saying either of the good's most serious competitors, the true and the beautiful. The great contribution of the Jews was in ethics, not aesthetics. It was in morality, not philosophy. In all biblical history there is only one example of anything that was exceptionally beautiful, the temple. And there is not one example of a philosopher. Beauty and truth were left to the Greeks.

Truth in the philosophical sense is not even mentioned in the earliest Gospels. The word *beauty* is used only twice in the New Testament. "Beauty is truth," Keats wrote, "truth beauty. That is all / ye know on earth, and all ye need to know." That is a Greek sentiment, not a Judeo-Christian one, and it is not coincidental that it is found in Keats's "Ode on a Grecian Urn."

An equally fine summary of the Judeo-Christian way is from one denomination's documents. "Truth," wrote the Presbyterians, "is in order to goodness." We know the truth in order to do the good. In the Judeo-Christian way of looking at life, truth without goodness is falsehood.

The goodness requirement sprang from controversy. "The LORD has a controversy with his people," Micah wrote (Mic. 6:2). *Controversy* was a legal term. It meant that God was bringing suit against Israel. Why? Because Israel had failed to do justice, love kindness, and walk humbly with its God. The consequences were dire. They had become vulnerable to foreign attack, and they were engaged in unparalleled domestic corruption.

God's controversy with us is that we make goodness controversial. We turn requirement into suggestion. "Do," "love," and "walk" are orders. A theology of action is the only one that has ever made sense to Christians and Jews.

To the extent that we do not do justice, love kindness, and walk humbly with our God, we become vulnerable to corruption and defeat. When we find ourselves doing them, however, it is God in action. It is grace.

PRAYER

Thank you for showing me what is good and moving me to do it. Amen.

HOW TO HEAL THE SICK

They went up on the roof and let him down...
through the tiles.

LUKE 5:19

Of the 3,799 verses in the Gospels, 727 are on healing. That's almost twenty percent of the verses. In
one instance, a paralyzed man is let down through a roof
to be healed by Jesus.

The impact of Jesus can make us instantly creative.
Who would have thought to drop the man through the
roof? In the houses of the day, beams were laid from wall
to wall, and between the beams twigs and branches were
mortised with clay. The men had to walk up the outside

of the house, where the stairs were, pull up the twigs and branches, then lower their friend through.

What can we do for a loved one or friend who is sick? We are limited only by our imaginations. But Jesus sets our imaginations free. We can telephone, visit, write, feed, babysit, transport, and send pictures, music, and jokes. Once in a hospital room I saw a portable radio with an orange bow. Someone had brought it so the patient could listen to her favorite programs on National Public Radio.

The impact of Jesus can also make us persistent. The paralyzed man's friends weren't going to let a packed house deter them. They would stop at nothing to get their friend to the healer. Jesus is impressed. Luke says "when he saw their faith," specifically including the friends, the healing occurred (Luke 5:20).

It is the people who come back to visit the patient who are like the friends of the paralyzed man. Especially if the illness is a long one, it is the people who persist in their attention who count. So often the patient is simply neglected and ultimately forgotten.

Or avoided. "I just can't go," we say to ourselves. "I might catch something. I might see death. I might face my own death." When we go, it has to be grace impelling us to go. How do we know? Because we won't go on our own.

How do we know? Because we haven't!

But if we persist so much that we find ourselves praying, then the patient can't be forgotten. We can even pray with the patient. "The prayer of faith will save the sick," an early Christian wrote (James 5:15). "When Jesus saw *their* faith." When the sick person sees our faith, it can only help the healing.

A doctor friend is a medical missionary to Costa Rica. He prays with every patient he treats. "There is more than one medicine," he says.

PRAYER

Give me the creativity and persistence I need to reach out to those who are ill. Amen.

HOW TO BE HUMBLE

He...began to wash the disciples' feet.
JOHN 13:5

J esus and his disciples were having dinner when Jesus "laid aside his garments, and girded himself with a towel. Then he poured water into a basin, and began to wash the disciples' feet" (John 13:4-5). The leader became the servant. It is a startling image of humility.

It is all the more remarkable when you realize what was going on at the time. Jesus knew he had provoked the authorities. He knew his time was short. He knew he could be arrested, tried, and killed at any moment. Still, he had time to wash his disciples' feet. It was a powerful image of putting first things first.

Jesus had the further concern of betrayal by one of his closest friends, a man whose ability and character were so revered they had made him treasurer of the group. Yet Jesus would wash Judas's feet, too. He would be a servant even of the one who would kill him.

As if the above were not enough, the group was bickering. They were arguing at the Last Supper about who would be first (Luke 22:24). To the end, they were competitive, proud, lusting for precedence. In the footwashing, Jesus was demonstrating the opposite. It was a powerful image of putting last things last, namely, the ego.

How can we be like Jesus? We can't, not on our own. We can't will humility. We can't will servanthood. It is too much to ask of the ego. It is too unnatural. The ego is too much with us, too powerful. We need images like this one of the kneeling Jesus to counteract the regal images we have of ourselves.

But can a simple image of a kneeling man do that for us? Yes—if we are ready for it, if we have been readied for it by the adding up of events. Then we can be surprised by grace. Then the image can work. Then we can see that grace has been at work all along in the events that brought us to this moment. Otherwise the Bible's images of humility will not work. They will be irrelevant. But when the timing is right, the Word of God always connects.

PRAYER

Help me see the kneeling Jesus washing my feet. Amen.

HOW TO DEAL WITH PRIDE

Blessed are the meek.

MATTHEW 5:5

Humility is one of the cardinal Christian virtues. Unfortunately, most of us are unable to be humble. We have to be humbled by what happens to us, either positive or negative. It could be a promotion—or a pink slip.

"Blessed are the meek," Jesus said, but meekness is not a virtue that comes willingly. There is no will in it. We can't will humility. We are too proud. It is our original sin. We are like the Greeks for whom humility was not a classical virtue. "Man is the measure of all things," Protagoras said. "What is man," the Bible asks, "that thou art mindful of him?" (Ps. 8:4).

The two major sources of pride in the Bible are wealth and power. Both should be sources of humility instead. As the Bible says: "Beware lest you say in your heart, 'My power and the might of my hand have gotten me this wealth.' You shall remember the LORD your God, for it is he who gives you power to get wealth" (Deut. 8:17-18).

The problem with wealth and power and other positive happenings like promotions is that they feed the ego and feelings of independence rather than feed the soul and feelings of dependence. That is why we say that, when we find ourselves being humbled, it has to be grace; it can't be us. Grace is whatever humbles us.

Most often, human nature being what it is, humility appears when a so-called *negative* event brings us low. Curiously, the word *humility* comes from the root *humus,* meaning "earth." We are brought down to earth by events that humble us.

We find God close to the earth rather than towering above it. That is to say, God finds us there. High places in the Bible are often denigrated because they are prideful, from the Tower of Babel to the cedars of Lebanon.

Humility is one way divinity reaches us. When we are knocked flat, laid low, brought down to earth, that is when, for perhaps the first time in life, we actually experience God.

PRAYER

Thank you for the events in my life that humble me.
Amen.

HOW TO LAUGH

---

*The disciples of John fast often and offer prayers ...
but yours eat and drink.*

LUKE 5:33

Jesus went to dinner parties and wedding feasts. He enjoyed himself so much that one of the charges against him was that he was "a glutton and a drunkard" (Luke 7:34). "The disciples of John fast often and offer prayers," his critics charged, "and so do the disciples of the Pharisees, but yours eat and drink."

He often used humor to twit the Pharisees. He used exaggeration, as when he said it was easier for a camel to go through the eye of a needle than for a rich man to get

162

into heaven. He used the absurd, as when he talked about casting pearls before swine. He used irony, as when he said that people who think their religion has to be dull "have received their reward" (Matt. 6:2).

He made up humorous parables, as the one about pouring new wine into old wineskins, to tease those who were saying, "That old-time religion is good enough for me." He joked with his friends, as when he called Simon "Peter," which meant "rock," knowing full well that the mercurial Peter was anything but stable, at least outwardly.

There are more than five hundred puns in the Old Testament, over two hundred in the New. Far from being "the lowest form of humor," punning to the ancients was considered high humor. "Then the LORD God formed man *[adam]* of dust from the ground *[adamah]*" (Gen. 2:7). Adam blames Eve, Eve blames the serpent—humorous touches.

Laughter is a hallmark of the faith. At least it should be. A dour Christian is a contradiction in terms. "His disciples should look more redeemed," Nietzsche said. I have a poster of a laughing Jesus, head thrown back, roaring with laughter. It's an image we never see and never even think about seeing. But Jesus was fully human as well as fully divine, and that meant he experienced the full range of human emotions, including laughter. Moved by grace, we can see ourselves with heads thrown back. It would have to be grace because we don't view our faith as a laughing matter.

Is it any wonder that Jesus emphasized joy in his last conversation with his disciples? "These things I have spoken to you," he said, "that my joy may be in you, and that your joy may be full" (John 15:11). Even in the face of his imminent death, he wanted to leave them on a note of joy. It was a note they would continue to sound as they faced their own deaths. "Without having seen him you love him," Peter wrote his fellow Christians during Nero's persecution, "and rejoice with unutterable and exalted joy" (1 Pet. 1:8).

PRAYER

Help me experience the joy of my faith with the image of a laughing Jesus. Amen.

HOW TO AVOID DROWNING

Noah walked with God.

GENESIS 6:9

A flood can come at any time—an actual flood or a flood of failure, loss, illness, grief, hurt. Water can cleanse, but it can also rot. It can transport, but it can also sink. It can create life, but it can also drown.

The two sides of water are in each of us, which means they are also in the Bible. On the one hand, the Bible has a dim view of human nature. "Every imagination of the thoughts of his heart," the Bible says, "was only evil continually" (Gen. 6:5). So God decides to destroy humanity with a flood, saying "I am sorry that I have made them" (Gen. 6:7).

On the other hand, there was Noah. "Noah walked with God." His imagination was anything but evil. For some reason, Noah was able to imagine God on the other side of the flood.

How can we imagine God on the other side of our floods? One answer is in the Bible's declaration that "Noah walked with God." If we walk with God in the good times, we can walk with God in the bad.

One way to walk with God is to collect images of God from the Bible. We don't choose to collect. We don't choose to read the Bible. It may have long been un-opened. We are impelled to read the Bible. The impulsion is grace.

Is this not a tired answer, to read the Bible? No. How else can we walk with God if we do not imagine God? And how can we imagine God without the Bible? "Imagination," Einstein said, "is more important than knowledge." We don't know the outcome when we are being flooded with images brought on by failure, loss, illness, grief, hurt. But we can imagine the outcome by receiving images of God through them.

Noah walked with God before the flood, so he was able to imagine God in the flood. Noah was 950 years old when he died, 600 when the flood came. It is the Bible's way of saying, "Take your time. Don't push the river. Your images of God are working their way in you."

Grace is what enables us to take our time.

PRAYER

Help me imagine you in my flood. Amen.

HOW TO HANDLE A
PROBLEM AT WORK

You must bear witness also at Rome.
ACTS 23:11

We can have a seemingly impossible problem at work or at home, and it can affect everything we do. "I even have trouble getting out of bed in the morning," a friend said. His particular problem was a work problem. It seemed impossible to solve.

Such all-consuming problems are gracious invitations to what we can't do, to what we can't self-help our way out of. They can be gifts, giving us the rest of who we are, the part of ourselves we have not yet experienced, the part where the power of God is, Paul's "inmost self" (Rom. 7:22), grace.

Paul was in an impossible situation, arguing for his life, with a mob about to kill him. At that point, grace brought an image of Jesus. "The ... Lord stood by him and said, 'Take courage ... you must bear witness also at Rome.'" The new world of Rome was being opened to Paul at the very moment he found himself in an impossible situation.

Similarly, the new world of passivity—of not being self-reliant—was being opened to my friend with the job problem. He was being given the gift of a whole other side of himself, his passive side, to complement his active side, the can-do side that could solve all its problems. "You mean," he said, "that I am learning humility?"

One way or another, we have to experience passivity, whose agent is grace, or we will never be fully alive. Impossible problems can only be solved by grace. My friend had tried everything to deal with his impossible problem, from talking to the people at work to reading self-help books to getting counseling. "Nothing seems to work," he told me, his head in his hands.

What my friend was learning was that, whatever problem we are given in life, it is the problem we have to be given in order to discover the rest of who we are, our passive side that can experience the remarkable power of grace. Our impossible problem is the crucifixion we have to go through to be raised to new life. We are "raised"; we do not "raise ourselves."

"If any one is in Christ," Paul wrote, "he is a new creation" (2 Cor. 5:17 NRSV). We are "in Christ" as we undergo our particular crucifixion. Resurrection comes as we find ourselves on the road to our particular Rome. My friend found himself leaving his job, starting a new one, enjoying life, and giving all credit to grace.

PRAYER

When nothing seems to work, show me what will. Amen.

HOW TO HANDLE
INADEQUACY

I do not know how to speak, for I am only a youth.
JEREMIAH 1:6

Most of us feel inadequate at one time or another. We may even feel inadequate most of our lives. It can begin as early as childhood. God says to Jeremiah, "I appointed you a prophet to the nations" (Jer. 1:5). But Jeremiah quickly responds, "Ah, Lord God! Behold, I do not know how to speak, for I am only a youth."

Of course he was too young. Of course he was inexperienced. Of course he had no idea what to say. His total inadequacy would be the proof that it was God speaking through him. When people heard him they would hear God. "Behold," God says, "I have put my words in your mouth" (Jer. 1:9).

Of course we are not adequate. We were never expected to be adequate. Grace has to make us adequate. God comes into view as we find ourselves becoming adequate to God's assignments. What is God's assignment for me? It is likely something for which I feel completely inadequate.

If we were adequate to God's tasks, there would be no need for God.

All the calls in the Bible come to people who feel inadequate. Sarah laughs at what she is called to do (Gen. 18:12). Moses argues over his assignment: "Who am I that I should go to Pharaoh?" (Exod. 3:11). Gideon protests that his clan is the weakest, and he is the least in his family (Judg. 6:15). God gives him the only possible response. "But I will be with you" (Judg. 6:16).

That is all we need to know, that God will be with us as we obey our calls.

And, since we are completely inadequate to the task, all credit will be God's. People will see and hear God because of us.

Are we called to a certain job? A certain spouse? A service project? Running for office? Sharing the Bible? A picket line? Organizing a church? Or maybe even called to go home and play with our children for a change?

When will we set about doing what we can't not do? When we are ready. And when will that be? We will know. The events of life will come together and move us to fulfill our assignment. For Jeremiah it was as simple an event as seeing a rod of almond and a boiling pot (Jer. 1:11, 13). They were enough to get him to prophesy.

So we should take heart if we are feeling inadequate because God is calling us in our inadequacy to do something in which others will see God.

PRAYER

Thank you for speaking to me in places where I feel least capable. Amen.

HOW TO LIVE FROM THE INSIDE OUT

You . . . outwardly appear righteous . . . but within
you are full of hypocrisy.

MATTHEW 23:28

The Pharisees received some of Jesus' strongest criticism. One reason was that they lived from the outside in rather than from the inside out.

Living from the outside in is when the most important thing in life is success or fame or money or power. The Pharisees had all four. Those things that should have been secondary had become primary.

Living from the outside in is when we are still blaming our parents for our problems. It is when we are not being all we could be. Our stress is the clue that we are living more externally than internally, more from the outside in than from the inside out.

Jesus, of course, offers the best example of living from the inside out. He could break the rules and had his priorities straight. He told us as well as showed us how to live from the inside out. It's all there in the Sermon on the Mount (Matt. 5–7), the key to which is "seek first his kingdom and his righteousness, and all these things shall be yours as well" (Matt. 6:33).

Our ability to live from the inside out comes from grace. We are too pharisaical to live that way on our own. We don't seek first the Kingdom. Only grace can move us to seek it first, and then only for a short while. We have to be moved by grace again and again.

PRAYER

Help me live from the inside out. Amen.

HOW TO BE INSPIRED

When the day of Pentecost had come, they were all together in one place.

ACTS 2:1

One of the best arguments for joining a church is that the experience can be inspiring. Yes, you can be inspired outside the church, as was St. Paul. But Paul was the exception that proves the rule. There is no other solo experience of the Holy Spirit in the New Testament.

"They were all together in one place." That was why they were inspired. People in churches are all together in worship, in prayer groups, Bible groups, youth groups, couples groups, singles groups, seniors groups, and service groups. Something happens to us in a group that doesn't happen when we are alone.

Jesus brought each of the disciples into a small group. By the time of his death, the group of twelve had grown to one hundred twenty (Acts 1:15). Jesus knew that people needed one another to remain strong in the faith. The point of creating a church was to enable people to experience together what they might not experience alone. Pentecost happened to a group, not to an individual.

I like to think that Jesus needed the group himself and that it was not formed solely for the purpose of propagating the faith. He needed it for his faith. Otherwise, he could simply have wandered around Galilee as an itinerant teacher with no concern for building a following. He needed them as much as they needed him.

It is unfortunate that, when people join a church, they are not immediately placed in a group. They are offered any number of groups, but they are never expected to join one as a condition of membership. Consequently, you have a lot of people wandering out of churches after having been in them only a few months or years. They were never fully integrated into the life of the parish, because they never had the Pentecostal experience of the power of the group.

One way to prevent such an exodus is to keep together each group of new members when they join. Led by the pastor or lay person until they can be on their own, the group is shown how to pray, read the Bible, share life experiences, and do service projects together.

In this way, they can experience the same inspiration, the same indwelling of the Holy Spirit, that the first-century church experienced. It can be one of the most powerful experiences of grace they will ever have. Proof is the explosive proliferation of groups that formed the first-century church.

PRAYER

May I be led by the Spirit to a discipleship group in my church. Amen.

HOW TO HANDLE
INTERRUPTIONS

They followed Jesus.

JOHN 1:37

Andrew and John were standing with John the Baptist when Jesus walked by. "Behold, the Lamb of God!" John exclaimed (John 1:36). "The two disciples heard him say this, and they followed Jesus." The sudden appearance of Jesus interrupted the course of their lives.

One of the things a Christian learns is that interruptions can be grace. But it is not an easy learning. When we have our week planned and an interruption disrupts our plan, we are at least disconcerted and at most angry.

The one evening I had planned to catch up on three days of desk work was interrupted by a call about an eighty-two-year-old who had come to town to share his particular road to discipleship. "When we see people through their mistakes," he said, "we immediately judge. When I see them through their needs, I immediately love."

"Love," this disciple said, "hears what is not said. Love the other person the way he or she needs to be loved, not the way you need to love. Love does not take for granted. Love has that note of celebration, of joy, of bubbling overflow." He told us how he had hidden seven 3x5 cards around his house for his wife, one for each day he was gone, and how the cards said, in one form or another, "I love you."

When someone drops unexpectedly into our lives, interrupting the day we had planned, it could be Jesus in the form of that person. Certainly, the old man with his message of love was an incarnation of Jesus that night for me.

PRAYER

Help me be opened to you by every interruption. Amen.

HOW TO RECONCILE

Return to your country and to your kindred.

GENESIS 32:9

We all have unfinished business. There is always someone with whom we are incomplete. Twenty years late, Jacob finds himself returning to face his brother, Esau, whose birthright he had stolen.

But Jacob was not returning on his own. Going back voluntarily to the one we have wronged is too much to expect. We have to have help. "O LORD who didst say to me, 'Return to your country and to your kindred.' " Grace was the help Jacob needed. Grace would send him back.

For twenty years he hadn't voluntarily gone back. Now he would be sent back.

So often we think of God as abstract, "out there," "up there," beyond us. But God is very much within us. "The kingdom of God is within you," Jesus said (Luke 17:21 KJV). Grace moves us to be complete with someone we have wronged.

Without grace our motivation just isn't there. The last thing we want to do is go back to the one we have wronged. So when we are moved to do so, we say it is grace motivating us. It moves us through our emotions.

Take Jacob's fear. "I fear him," he says of his brother (Gen. 32:11). Rightly so. We tend to avoid what we fear, so if we are propelled back into it, there has to be something beyond us working within us. Whenever we are moved into our fear instead of away from it, it has to be grace; it can't be us, because, left to our own devices, we haven't moved into our fear. But we are not left to our own devices. That is the message of the Bible.

"I will do you good," God says (Gen. 32:12). It is remarkable. Jacob breaks through to the goodness of God beyond the fear of his brother. "I fear him, lest he come and slay us all" (Gen. 32:11). There would be goodness even if there were death. We may fear dying, but if we are complete, if we have been moved to completion with one whom we have wronged, there can be a vision of goodness beyond our vision of fear.

"I am not worthy," Jacob says, "of the least of all the steadfast love and all the faithfulness which thou hast shown to thy servant" (Gen. 32:10). He has an appropriately humble attitude, as he finds himself propelled by grace to be complete with his brother. No humility means no completion. Only when I am humbled will I be able to see that I am a servant, unable to reconcile on my own, led to reconcile, by grace.

PRAYER

Move me to completion with the one I have wronged.
Amen.

HOW TO BE A LEADER

Moses rose with his servant Joshua, and ... went up into the mountain.

EXODUS 24:13

If we want to be leaders, we might take a look at Joshua. What did Joshua have that made him Moses' successor rather than someone else?

For one thing, grace had given him a feel for God. He was "a man in whom is the spirit" (Num. 27:18). Of all the people, it is Joshua who is with Moses on the mountain of God, and it is Joshua who is with him when he comes off the mountain and sees the Golden Calf (Exod.

184

24:13; 32:17). Moses knew that Joshua had a feel for God that none of the others had. It was perceptive of Moses. It was good mentoring.

We all have our ups and downs. We all are tossed about by the vicissitudes of life. But we all know people who, in spite of all that is going on in their lives, have a feel for the center. They have an inner gyroscope. Often it is because they are people "in whom is the spirit." Grace has given them a serenity. Grace is their gyroscope.

Joshua had a feel for God. Emotion often precedes thought in matters of faith. Whatever we think about, we have first felt about. We think about it because it engages us emotionally. Even a scientist, who is the acme of cool, logical thinking, finds himself or herself working on a particular scientific problem because he or she has a feel for it. It is exciting, enjoyable, fun.

Percept precedes concept. We perceive God before we conceive God. Grace gives us a feel for God before we have an idea of God. We have a hunch before we have a thought. God is emotional before God is rational. That is why the logic of theology means nothing to those who have not already had some experience of God. Creeds mean nothing to those for whom God has not already meant everything.

Joshua was chosen because Moses sensed he was in touch with God. He knew Joshua had his center, and he knew that Joshua's center was outside himself. Grace gives us a center outside ourselves. There was more to Joshua than his own ego. Moses knew Joshua would be a good leader and could bring the people through whatever might befall them. Our graceful center can do the same for us.

PRAYER

Help me find the center my life in you. Amen.

HOW TO ENJOY CHURCH

*That my joy may be in you, and that your joy may
be full.*

JOHN 15:11

You couldn't keep those first Christians down. Their communions were joyful, as they "celebrated" the resurrection. Their fellowship was rich, warm, enthusiastic, full of the Spirit. Joy is one of the clearest indicators of grace.

"Each one has a hymn," Paul wrote, "a lesson, a revelation, a tongue, or an interpretation" (1 Cor. 14:26). Their worship was joyful.

It was the Pharisees who drained the fun out of

religion. Maybe that was why Jesus was always confronting them. They were too serious about their faith. They had cut the spontaneity from life.

I was with a group of Christians who were laughing and singing. You could feel the enthusiasm. *Enthusiasm* comes from the root for "God within." Among other things, the group was praying, and when the prayer was over, there was joy on their faces and even tears of joy in some eyes. It was "God within," all right.

The first Christians laughed. They sang. Their faith was fresh, new, exciting. Is it any wonder that we "celebrate" the communion? Why, then, are virtually all communions joyless?

If we're in a church that isn't full of joyous people, then we may be in the wrong church. More to the point, we may be in a church that is a contradiction in terms. A holy place is a joyful place.

PRAYER

Thank you for the gift of joy. May our church be a holy and joyful place. Amen.

HOW TO BE TRANSPORTED
BY JOY

*May the God of hope fill you with all joy and peace
in believing.*
ROMANS 15:13

It was during a worship service. We were singing, sway-
ing, clapping. The joy was palpable. We had lost track
of time. We were standing. We were "transported." We
were "caught up in the Spirit." We were experiencing the
"joy of the Lord." It was a pure manifestation of grace.

Joy is the second "fruit of the Spirit" in Paul's famous
list, right after love (Gal. 5:22). It is the chief characteristic
of grace. Who is the most joyful person you know? "May

the God of hope," Paul wrote, "fill you with all joy and peace in believing." A believer is joyful by definition.

The Greeks of Jesus' time believed that there was no such thing as pure joy. Joy was always tempered by anxiety. An overabundance of happiness, the Greeks said, would call down the envy of the gods.

But for the Christians, joy was a gift of God. Indeed, we are reminded that the very words *joy, grace, gift* had the same root in the Greek of the day. The grace of God, which was the gift of God, brought the joy of God. Joy is what happens when we are released from space and time by grace.

One way grace operates is through the Holy Spirit. Jesus patiently explained to his disciples that his death would not leave them desolate but would bring them the Holy Spirit (John 14:16-17, 26). He even said "it is to your advantage that I go away, for if I do not go away, the Counselor will not come to you" (John 16:7).

When did we last forget what time it was? When did we last feel "transported"? It is at such times that we may experience this fruit of the Spirit. The inspired early Christians, those with the "Spirit within," were joyful. "These things I have spoken to you," Jesus said, "that my joy may be in you, and that your joy may be full" (John 15:11).

PRAYER

Thank you for joy in believing. Help me lose myself in the joy of worshiping you. Amen.

HOW TO EXPERIENCE JOY
IN SUFFERING

Count it all joy...when you meet various trials.

JAMES 1:2

It is hard to understand, but those first Christians some-how experienced joy in spite of their suffering. They took their lead from Jesus, "who for the joy that was set before him endured the cross" (Heb. 12:2). The promise of joy on the other side of death enabled the first Christians to be joyful while they faced their own deaths.

"You joyfully accepted the plundering of your property," an awed early Christian wrote, "since you knew that you yourselves had a better possession and an abiding one" (Heb. 10:34). It was extraordinary. It was grace.

Joy was a recurrent theme in Paul's letter to the Philippians, a letter made all the more remarkable when we remember that it was Paul's last letter, written just before he would likely be killed. Peter, during Nero's persecution, when Christians were being "tested by fire," exclaims that his readers "rejoice with unutterable and exalted joy" (1 Pet. 1:8). It was incredible.

Life with Christ is a matter of the joy as well as what Dietrich Bonhoeffer called the "cost of discipleship." Indeed, the cost is transformed into joy. "I rejoice in my sufferings," Paul writes, because "in my flesh I complete what is lacking in Christ's afflictions for the sake of his body, that is, the church" (Col. 1:24).

When we view our suffering as completing Christ's, and when we view it as a witness to others on behalf of Jesus, that casts suffering in a whole new light. The famed death-researcher Elisabeth Kübler-Ross, after years of examining the evidence from dying people, added joy to her five stages of dying: denial, anger, bargaining, despair, acceptance, and joy.

Surprised by Joy is the title of C. S. Lewis's autobiography. He had known plenty of suffering, including the loss of the woman he loved. But, being a Christian, he was able to break through to joy in spite of his suffering. More accurately, joy was able to break through to him. It was sheer grace.

PRAYER

Help me feel the joy the first Christians felt, even in the midst of suffering. Amen.

HOW TO LISTEN FOR GOD

What are you doing here, Elijah?

1 KINGS 19:9

Prayer is two-way. We're good at the one-way but less good at the two-way. We talk, but we don't listen. When there is no answer in the silence, we give up. We wonder, would the God of the universe say something to me?

One of the words for "pray" in the Bible comes from the root for "incline toward." The image is that of a deaf person inclining toward someone who is speaking. It is how Elijah hears the "still small voice" (1 Kings 19:12).

Elijah inclines toward God to catch God's response to what he has said.

More boldly still, the original sense of this word for "pray" was to "stroke the face." As a child leans forward to catch a parent's word, the child strokes the parent's cheek. To pray is to stroke God's cheek.

"What are you doing here, Elijah?" God asks. The still small voice was giving him the large, loud command to get on with the job he had to do. He was to come off the mountain where he was praying and carry the divine word to Syria.

We have to see a change in our behavior, or we haven't prayed, not yet. Our prayer is still one-way and therefore only halfway. We may have spoken, but we haven't listened. We haven't heard, obeyed, acted. We need grace to power us through praying to listening.

How are we to hear what we are to do? The case of Elijah is instructive. He had gone from the height of success, beating four hundred and fifty prophets in a contest, to the depth of despair, in flight from the prophets' patron, Queen Jezebel. It was as he hid in a cave on Mt. Horeb that he heard God speak. But it was also as he beat the prophets on Mt. Carmel that he had heard God speak.

We hear God on the heights and in the depths of life. It is on our mountains and in our caves that we find ourselves reaching up to stroke the face of God. At last, we find ourselves in two-way prayer. Apparently, there have to be huge emotions, such as elation and despair, to get us to listen. The only trouble is, in the elation, we tend to forget God, and in the despair, we tend to think God has forgotten us. That is why it can only be grace when we hear.

PRAYER

Help me know that in my elation and my despair you are there. Amen.

HOW TO HANDLE
SUPERFICIALITY

*He rose and went to a lonely place, and there he
prayed.*

MARK 1:35

Mark gives us a vivid image of Jesus at prayer: "In the morning, a great while before day, he rose and went to a lonely place, and there he prayed."

Where is our lonely place? It could be anywhere in our house or apartment or even in the car or on the bus or train to work. There is no better way to start or finish the day than with prayer.

Unfortunately, the rhythm of life for many of us is from the outside in. Breakfast, car, job, family, sleep—all fine, make no mistake. It's just that they need to be complemented by the rhythm of life from the inside out— lonely place, breakfast, car, job, family, lonely place, sleep.

What happens in the lonely place? We get in touch with the deepest part of who we are. What is that part? The image of God. "Let us make man in our image," God says at creation (Gen. 1:26). A tree grows from the inside out. We can trace the growth in the rings.

We, too, can grow from the inside out, from where God is, into what we can become. Hopefully, our growth can be traced in the prayer rings. If there are no prayer rings, we may never grow into what is in us to become, fully alive. Instead, we are content to live a superficial life.

Whenever we find ourselves in a lonely place, grace is what draws us. As Jesus pointed out, in a thought that doubtlessly came from a lonely place: "No one can come to me unless drawn by the Father who sent me" (John 6:44 NRSV).

To what lonely place are we drawn?

PRAYER

Thank you for drawing me to my lonely place. Amen.

HOW TO HANDLE LOSS

Take your son, your only son Isaac, whom you love.

GENESIS 22:2

God tells Abraham to kill his own son. It is a test of faith. God will stay Abraham's hand, but Abraham doesn't know that. This is the same God who sends Satan after Job (Job 1:12), tests Jesus with temptations (Matt. 4:1), and crushes the Suffering Servant (Isa. 53:10).

It is the dark side of God. "Truly, thou art a God who hides thyself," Isaiah says (Isa. 45:15). The inscrutable God commits inscrutable acts. But this is the same God who says, "I will give you the treasures of darkness" (Isa. 45:3). There are treasures here on the dark side of God.

We discover the treasures of darkness in what is called the "dark night of the soul," when dark events fall into our lives and the light of understanding is out and we can't find our way. We are so "in the dark" about what has happened to us that we even say God caused it to happen.

In the midst of our retirement, our spouse dies. In the midst of our good grades in college, we get a D. In the midst of our engagement, we realize this is the wrong person. The events of life are constantly tempting us to give up on God. But if grace can move us to see treasures in darkness, then we can find ourselves not giving up.

"When it is dark enough," Goethe said, "you can see the stars." It is at that moment, in our crisis, that the hidden God can appear and the dark God be brought to light. At the moment Abraham took the knife to slit his son's throat, God stayed his hand. Because it was at that point, the darkest moment in Abraham's life, that Abraham's love for God over everything else was made clear.

Can we lose the thing we love the most and not lose God? The story of Abraham and Isaac is saying that if we love anything more than we love God, we don't have faith. We may have belief. We may be able to say the Apostles' Creed. We may be able to sing the hymns and say the prayers. But we don't have faith. More accurately, faith doesn't have us. Grace has not brought it yet. "By grace you have been saved through faith" (Eph. 2:8).

Grace views everything we love the most—from spouse to children to job to life itself—as gifts rather than as givens. That means we can lose any of them and still remain fast to the giver. But only if we have been moved by grace to absorb the meaning of such dark stories as those of Abraham, Job, and the Suffering Servant.

PRAYER

Help me see the light of your presence in my dark times.
Amen.

HOW TO HANDLE BEING LOST

I have found my sheep which was lost.

LUKE 15:6

We are like the lost sheep of Jesus' story. We have wandered off the faithful path. We have lost our way. We have "followed too much the devices and desires of our own hearts," as the old Anglican prayer says.

But how can we be found until we are lost? And how can we know we are lost until we are in a crisis? And what is a crisis but a gift to remind us we have been lost and to show us how we can be found?

202

When we go to the hospital, for instance, we are being put in touch with the lost part of ourselves. We are out of control. Events are beyond us. Everything is done for us not by us. In such a crisis, we are being healed, made whole. In theological language, we are being saved. Our crisis is bringing our savior.

All along we had pursued our own interest. It was fine as far as it went. We were the best and the brightest at work. We had a wonderful family. We served faithfully at church and in our local political party.

Then something happened that we couldn't control. Our spouse left. Our job disappeared. Whatever it was, we found we couldn't save ourselves. We had clearly lost our way. In order to find it again, we would have to be found. We would have to be slung over the shoulders of the shepherd and carried back to the fold.

Of course, we do not have to go to the hospital to be found by our shepherd. Things are happening daily over which we have no control. Each one is separating us from our ego, which is the best thing that could be happening to us if we want to be fully alive.

The ego gets us only so far in life. Then we have to move beyond it. We have to be moved beyond it. Crises, small and large, move us beyond ego, since the ego will never move itself. Each crisis is a gift of grace.

The sheep was incomplete without the shepherd. The ego is incomplete without the alter ego. The active life is

Practical Grace

incomplete without the passive. What we do is incomplete without what can be done through us. Grace is our access to this new dimension.

Without grace, our access is blocked to the dimension of being fully alive. Grace comes in the form of our crises. They remind us that God is searching for us as our shepherd and that, when we are lost, we will be found.

PRAYER

Help me realize that you are reaching me through what I can't control. Amen.

204

HOW TO LOVE JESUS

Simon, son of John, do you love me?

JOHN 21:16

Jesus is not so much the head of my life as the heart of my life. The heart is central. That's why we say "the heart of the matter" rather than "the head of the matter." "Simon, son of John," Jesus asks Peter, "do you love me?" He does not ask, "Simon, do you believe in me?" The heart of the matter in Christianity is love, not thought. Loving Jesus is central, not thinking about him.

Christianity is a relationship, not an idea. This is not to say we do not think about Christ. Clearly, we do. But thinking about Christ and loving Jesus are two different things. If loving doesn't complement thinking, our faith will falter. If thinking doesn't complement loving, our faith will not necessarily falter.

Just as there is a love chapter in the Bible, 1 Corinthians 13, so, we have seen, there is a faith chapter, Hebrews 11. Abraham "went out," the author says, "not knowing where he was to go" (Heb. 11:8). It was the essence of faith. The faith was in the relationship, not in the thought. He had a relationship with God rather than a thought about God. His relationship was a gift of grace, just as the "love of my life," my spouse, is a gift of grace.

"Her sins, which are many, are forgiven," Jesus says of the woman who came to him, "for she loved much" (Luke 7:47). She had a big heart. It would mean something different if we said she had a big head. If we come to Christ because he makes sense, we will stay with him only because we love him.

"Christ Jesus has made me his own," Paul wrote (Phil. 3:12). Like Peter and the nameless woman and Abraham, Paul was in a relationship. And it was a particular kind of relationship, one in which the loved one had graciously taken the initiative. It was also a relationship that would see him through whatever adversity he might encounter. He was writing from jail, awaiting execution.

"I have learned the secret," he writes. "I can do all

things in him who strengthens me" (Phil. 4:12-13). The secret was love.

PRAYER

May I love you with the fervor of Paul, your great intellectual.
Amen.

HOW TO MEDITATE

I will meditate on all thy work.

PSALM 77:12

One way to get closer to God is to meditate. The psalmist says he will meditate on God's work. Presumably, that will bring him close to God, and, if he is lucky, he may even experience God directly.

The direct experience of God is what we are all after, but few of us are willing to go through what looks like the hard work of meditating as one way to have that experience. Our days are so fast-paced that we have no time to sit quietly, banish all thoughts, and wait patiently for God.

Something has to happen to us to get us to meditate. High blood pressure, perhaps. Or it may be the pressure of events. Our fast pace may catch up with us, and we may suddenly realize that life is too short not to experience all that we can before we die.

Or it may be that something deeply troubling has to happen to us to get us to meditate. That may have been the way it was for the psalmist. "In the day of my trouble," he writes, "I seek the Lord...I meditate" (Ps. 77:2-3).

More accurately, he finds himself meditating. He didn't will it. But now events have caught up with him. "I cry aloud to God...that he may hear me" (Ps. 77:1). His cry is grace. Grace is reaching him through his trouble.

Any of these verses would be a good one on which to meditate. We can let the verse seep into our consciousness for twenty minutes or so. "The poverty of the single verse," John Cassian put it, an early writer on spirituality. Finding the verse is itself an act of grace. We say we were "led" to it.

We may even bring a single verse down to a single word, such as *Jesus*. The sustained rhythm of the single word and our breathing takes us into a deeper level of consciousness. That is why even high blood pressure can be considered a gift. We call it a gift of grace.

PRAYER

Thank you for whatever gets me thinking of you. Amen.

HOW TO LEAD A
BALANCED LIFE

Do you believe this?

JOHN 11:26

It is important to rehabilitate the "Martha" side in each of us, as there has always been a tendency to disparage it because of the Mary and Martha story.

It is explicitly stated by John that Jesus loved both Mary and Martha, and he states it by referring to "Martha and her sister" (John 11:5). Luke says that it was Martha who owned the house, not Mary and not both of them together, thus giving Martha a status that is usually overlooked (Luke 10:38).

John also points out how it was Martha who was sufficiently undistracted in her bereavement to be able to go out and meet Jesus on his approach to Bethany and explain the situation regarding their brother, Lazarus, who had just died—while Mary sat home in despair (John 11:20).

Then, because of the impact of Jesus in their lives, Mary and Martha switch roles. "I am the resurrection and the life," Jesus says to Martha. "Do you believe this?" (John 11:25-26). "Yes, Lord," she replies, "I believe that you are the Christ, the Son of God" (John 11:27). It is Martha who makes the great inward statement of belief.

And it is Mary who does the great outward act of caring. "It was Mary," John writes, "who anointed the Lord with ointment and wiped his feet with her hair" (John 11:2).

Both sisters have integrated their opposites. The caregiver is the believer, and the believer is the caregiver. How do we achieve integration? One way is finding ourselves moved by grace to pray. To pray is to reflect on whether we are so inward-directed, as Mary, that we do not move out, or so outward-directed, as Martha, that we do not move in.

Prayer keeps us in touch with whether our lives are, at the moment, the day, the week, unbalanced, "distracted" in Luke's word (Luke 10:40). Then prayer rights the balance, as grace gives us an image of Jesus to catalyze, at least for a moment, a more balanced life.

PRAYER

Without you it will be impossible for me to maintain my balance. Amen.

HOW TO RECOGNIZE GOD

Would that my lord were with the prophet.

2 KINGS 5:3

The person bringing God into our life may be the least likely source for God. God came to Naaman, the Syrian general, in the form of a "little maid" (2 Kings 5:2), a girl who had been captured by the Syrians in a raid on the Israelis and was now a servant of Naaman's wife.

An enemy, captive, slave, child—there was no less likely source of God, and yet the little maid was the one bringing God into Naaman's life. "Would that my lord were with the prophet who is in Samaria!" she said to Naaman's wife. "He would cure him of his leprosy."

God falls into our lives through the most unlikely intervenors. An elderly woman lay terminally ill in a retirement home. One day a woman appeared at her bedside, a woman she had never known before, a new resident at the home. Every day thereafter, the woman would reappear and talk to the sick woman and stroke her hand and rub her back and fix her hair and talk to her about God.

Who is the least likely person to bring God into your life? Someone you would normally shun? Someone you don't like? An employee? A child? Grace is constantly seeking us.

The little maid tells Naaman to go to the prophet for help, and he goes to Elisha "with his horses and chariots" (2 Kings 5:9). It's quite an image—the commanding general in full-dress regalia at the flap of the barefoot prophet's tent. And then Elisha, through an intermediary, not even coming to greet him, tells Naaman to "Go and wash in the Jordan seven times, and your flesh shall be restored, and you shall be clean" (2 Kings 5:10).

Naaman cannot believe what he has heard. That's often the way it is when God speaks. The last thing Moses wanted to do was what God was telling him to do. Even Jesus struggled in the garden with what he felt God was calling him to do.

When a least likely source gives us a least likely

message, we would do well to pay attention. It could be God calling. Naaman was healed.

PRAYER

Help me be open to the least likely source bringing me to you. Amen.

HOW NOT TO BE
WEIGHED DOWN

Have no anxiety about anything.

PHILIPPIANS 4:6

It is most interesting that when Jesus talks about being weighed down by the cares of life he puts it this way: "Take heed to yourselves lest your hearts be weighed down with dissipation and drunkenness and cares of this life" (Luke 21:34).

Self-indulgence is our vain attempt to recover the present moment, which has been stolen by anxiety. We will do anything to live now. We will drink to excess, work to excess, play to excess. "When I drink wine," wrote an ancient Greek poet, "my worries go to sleep."

Or we deal with anxiety by ignoring it. We will do anything not to feel what we are really feeling. John Updike wrote a stunner of a book in *Rabbit Run*. It's about the various runs a man makes to try to escape from the cares of his life.

Anxiety's job is to get us to rely on God rather than on self. Our coming to God is not inevitable, of course. We may have to go through a lot more anxiety—if, indeed, we come to God at all. That is why Jesus and Paul had to issue commands about anxiety. "Do not be anxious," Jesus said (Matt. 6:25). "Have no anxiety about anything," Paul told the Philippians. Remarkably, he said it while awaiting execution.

Equally remarkable is the fact that the early Christians saw their anxiety being turned into joy. "Rejoice," Peter says, "in so far as you share Christ's sufferings" (1 Pet. 4:13). It was unbelievable. "Rejoice in the Lord always," Paul writes, as he awaits certain death (Phil. 4:4). "That my joy may be in you," Jesus says before his arrest and death, "and that your joy may be full" (John 15:11).

Apparently, the way to handle anxiety is to watch grace handle it. That would be wildly impractical if we hadn't seen its effectiveness in the lives of the saints and Christ's life. When our anxiety is such that our own attempts to handle it prove futile, then it is just possible that the joy of the Lord may break through to us. Even a glimmer of joy in anxiety will be sheer grace.

PRAYER

Help me learn from my anxieties that they are bringing me to you. Amen.

HOW TO HUMANIZE THE
SYSTEM

Go back to Egypt.

EXODUS 4:19

L ove has two dimensions—one-to-one and group-to-group. We tend to remember the first and forget the second. We are good on the personal dimension of love, less good on the corporate.

It is one thing to take a basket of food to a needy family at Christmas. But it is another thing to organize our friends to work for needed changes in welfare legislation. It is one thing to visit a youth in a reformatory. It is quite another to organize a youth center to prevent the youth's going to the reformatory in the first place.

These are examples of the difference between social service and social action. Both are needed. Indeed, there may be no social action without social service. Biblical love goes beyond social service to social action. Love will do anything for love.

Biblical love, being powerful, uses power. *Power* is not a dirty word. It has been defined as the ability to make your voice heard in community decision-making. One way to humanize the system—that is, to make it more loving—is to give more people a voice in controlling their own destinies.

Moses was called by God to give the people a voice. He was sent back to Egypt to organize the people to humanize the system. Grace led him to do it. He would never have done it on his own. How do we know that? Because he never did it. He was too busy enjoying the good life with his job and his family.

We are often too busy enjoying the good life to humanize the system. Giving the people a voice in controlling their own destiny is presumably the point of democracy, a word coming from *power* and *people*. But we give the power up. We elect people to govern our destinies and then forget about those destinies ourselves. So the system can easily become dehumanized.

We need more Christians working out the biblical

love-ethic by organizing for better laws to make our social system more humane. The true test of grace is its ability to get us to care.

PRAYER

Help me organize for love. Amen.

HOW TO HANDLE
IMPATIENCE

I waited patiently for the LORD.

PSALM 40:1

We are impatient for the arrival of God, particularly in times of distress. "Evils have encompassed me without number," writes a psalmist (Ps. 40:12). But he was able to "wait patiently for the Lord" to rescue him.

Impatience is a gift bringing us God, but the gift will not be ours if we try to self-help our way out of impatience. A child became critically ill and was not expected to live. One day he said to his parents, "You are free to live this day." It became a byword for his family's church. It meant that we are free to accept what is happening to us, even the negative things such as impatience, or we are free to try to self-help our way out of them.

An old Indian tracker named Stalking Wolf taught two boys how to track. One lesson was to walk eight miles through a blizzard wearing only short pants. "The cold wind is your brother," the old Indian said. "You have treated him as your enemy."

Later, the one telling the story wrote: "I stopped resisting the cold. The result was instantaneous. The cold wind seemed to laugh through the pines. My coldness was gone."

Our negative emotions cannot hurt us if we are at one with them, if we stop resisting them. The cold wind of impatience is our brother. We have treated him as our enemy. But if we do not resist him, he will bring us into a broad, good place, where we are free to live this day.

Of course, it is not easy to wait out impatience. We have to have help. Our help is in the form of grace, which enables us to wait. When we find ourselves waiting, we know it is grace; it can't be us, because we won't wait.

Grace also uses our church, where we hear stories like the boy's and such sentences as "I waited patiently for the Lord." Here, too, church members wait patiently with us while we wait. It is their waiting with us that gives us the courage to wait.

"I could not have handled this two years ago," a man

said, speaking of a crisis in his life. "I would have been climbing the walls." What happened two years ago? He found himself sharing his negative emotions with a small group of people in his church. Grace had led him to join the group.

PRAYER

Help me wait patiently for you. Amen.

HOW TO HANDLE
UNHAPPINESS

Suddenly a light from heaven flashed about him.

ACTS 9:3

Paul was at a turning point. He was unhappy with himself, or he wouldn't have been killing people. Something had to change, but he was unable to make the change himself. Events would have to change him. In the meantime, he would simply live his life.

Paul was also taking his unhappiness out on other people. He took out on them what he should have been taking in to himself. "I persecuted this Way to the death," he would later confess (Acts 22:4).

We have an alarming tendency to take out on others what we like least in ourselves. Mostly we do it at home, but fellow employees, friends, neighbors, and even strangers are not exempt from our wrath—and all because we are unhappy with ourselves.

Fortunately, things changed for Paul on the road to Damascus. "Suddenly a light from heaven flashed about him," and he heard Jesus speaking to him. Apparently, his unhappiness with himself had reached the point where, at last, he could be reached by grace.

With grace now noticeably at work, we find ourselves doing what we are rather than being what we do. We are no longer caught up in the frenetic world of achieving. We get our identity from who we are, a Christian, not from what we do, our successes. Our achieving flows from our being. Is it any wonder that God, in the great revelation of the divine name to Moses, simply says, "I am who I am" (Exod. 3:14)?

Paul, the Pharisee, let the destination, being right with God, determine the journey. Paul the Christian let the journey, loving God, determine the destination. Pharisees had ends and means confused, which is what happens when the destination is more important than the journey. Very soon the end, being right with God, can justify the means, killing people.

"Love God," St. Augustine said, "and then do as you

please." It is one of the classic Christian statements. Loving God is not the goal of life; it is the point of life. It is not the end of life; it is the way of life. It is not something we strive for; it is something we do. Loving God is the journey, and it takes us wherever it takes us—to difficult assignments, as Paul, and, yes, to happiness.

PRAYER

Thank you for showing me the way to happiness. Amen.

HOW TO BE AT PEACE

They shall beat their swords into plowshares.

ISAIAH 2:4

Peace is as elusive as ever. In all the years of recorded history, only a few have known peace. No wonder Isaiah was quoted by the president of Egypt, Anwar Sadat, when he made his historic address to the Israeli parliament. It is also the quote chosen for the wall opposite the entrance to the United Nations building in New York. Sadat read:

> They shall beat their swords into plowshares,
> and their spears into pruning hooks;

nation shall not lift up sword against nation,
neither shall they learn war any more.

One road to peace is through Jesus. "Peace I leave
with you," he said to his disciples (John 14:27). "He is
our peace," an early Christian exclaimed (Eph. 2:14). Re-
flecting on Jesus had given him inner peace.

Because of Jesus, the early Christians found themselves
beating swords into plowshares. "There is neither Jew nor
Greek," an incredulous Paul found himself writing, "there
is neither slave nor free, there is neither male nor female;
for you are all one in Christ Jesus" (Gal. 3:28). All the
usual hostilities were broken down in Jesus. "He ... has
broken down the dividing wall of hostility" (Eph. 2:14).
The emancipation of women was advanced by the Christian religion.

Often peace within and peace between can happen
only through peace beyond. When peace happens, it is evidence for God. "The LORD ... has given peace to his people," David exulted (1 Chron. 23:25). "I make peace," the
Lord says (Isa. 45:7 KJV). "Thou dost keep him in perfect
peace," Isaiah explains, "whose mind is stayed on thee"
(Isa. 26:3).

If we will stay our minds on God, we will have
peace—first within us, then between us. But how do we
stay our minds on God? We don't. If we could, there
would be more peace. When peace happens, it has to be

grace; it can't be us, because we can't stay our minds on God.

When we find ourselves at peace—at home, work, or school—it is grace, God in action.

PRAYER

Thank you for my times of peace. Amen.

HOW TO EXPERIENCE
GOD'S POWER

Holy, holy, holy.

ISAIAH 6:3

We don't go to church because we want to. We go
because we have to. We can't stay away. It is the
power of God drawing us. It is God in action, grace.

We don't go to church to lead a better life. We don't
go to get peace of mind. We don't go to be happy. We go
to be jolted out of ourselves by the objective power of God.

If the service is a jolt, it will be as large a dose of the
power of God as we can take for one week. Of course,

many services aren't jolts, and the power of God doesn't get through, except for the fact that the church is there and the people are there, symbolizing the power.

Isaiah found himself pounded by the objective power of God in a worship service. "Holy, holy, holy," he hears. *Holy* in the Hebrew is from the root for "separate." God is what we are not. It is not what we do to God that counts, but what God does to us, objectively. Only God can overcome the separation between God and us.

The trouble begins when we say we can overcome the separation ourselves. No one is going to tell us we can't come near. And yet that is precisely what the objective power of God says: Stay back. No one shall touch my holy mountain (Exod. 19.12).

Then how do we get to the mountain? We don't. The mountain gets to us. But we are in church. We have come to the mountain. Not by our own volition. Subjectively we'd rather be home with the Sunday paper. We didn't come to church. We were brought to church—by the objective power of God. The objective beats the subjective.

"Holy, holy, holy." We are here because God brought us. No wonder "the foundations of the thresholds shook" (Isa. 6:4). It was the objective power of God manifesting in a worship service. A jolt.

PRAYER

May I find myself reminded each Sunday where my faith comes from. Amen.

HOW TO PRAY
VULNERABLY

The Spirit helps us in our weakness.
ROMANS 8:26

Praying is a new way of thinking. We don't come to it easily. We are trained to be logical, and here we are with our head in our hands. It doesn't make sense and is faintly embarrassing.

Beneath embarrassment is fear. We are afraid to be out of control.

Away from our usual mode of handling things, we get nervous. Prayer begins in the stomach, not in the head. It is emotional rather than intellectual.

Our growth occurs when we find ourselves out of control. It is often when we are least in control that we are most ourselves. Why? Because we have become vulnerable and therefore available—to the rest of who we are and to God.

How do we know the self is expanding and God is arriving? For one thing, we lose track of time. For another, we're not distracted. We're "there" as well as "lost." Everything is immediate. For still another, we come up slightly "intoxicated." That was how the first Christians were described after they prayed (Acts 2:13). I have yet to raise my head from a prayer group and not see a difference on people's faces.

What has happened? We have moved from the security of our head to the insecurity of our gut. Only we haven't done the moving. Grace has. We have been moved. We wouldn't have moved on our own. We prefer the safety of control to the risk of being out of control. That is why we say it is grace moving us to pray. "All that we have done," Isaiah says, "you have done for us" (Isa. 26:12 NRSV).

We find ourselves moving beyond talking to listening, beyond words to silence. In the silence Paul heard that "the Spirit helps us in our weakness; for we do not know how to pray as we ought, but the Spirit...intercedes for us."

Grace is the name that comes to us whenever we find

ourselves moving from reason to emotion, from logic to embarrassment, from control to fear. In a word, praying.

PRAYER

Thank you for the gift of the Spirit to help me in my weakness. Amen.

HOW TO PRAY
HELPLESSLY

*His sweat became like great drops of blood falling
down upon the ground.*

LUKE 22:42

When Jesus prayed in the garden of Gethsemane before his arrest, the Bible says that he was "in an
agony" and that he prayed until "his sweat became like
great drops of blood falling down upon the ground." He
needed all the help he could get at that point in his life. If
we need no help, we need no prayer.

It is the feeling of helplessness that often drives us to

pray. Hannah prayed wordlessly in the temple in her despair that she could not conceive a child (1 Sam. 1:13). After Jesus died, his leaderless followers prayed (Acts 1:14).

All we have to do in prayer is share our feelings, either out loud or in silence. Prayer is as much a matter of the heart as it is of the head. All God wants is who we are, and that means what we are feeling at any given moment.

But feelings are not always shared easily. We have our guard up much of the time. We are well defended. We are afraid to share who we are with others, even with those closest to us. So we are often out of practice when it comes to sharing our feelings with God.

But if we find ourselves persisting, prayer can work. It is those things we do most often that are the most important. We go to school, do our jobs, practice the piano. What we do most is what we value most. Grace inspires us to persist in prayer.

"My job is to pray," writes Archbishop Anthony Bloom, who is also a physician. "I leave the results to God." What a relief not to be results-oriented in one area of our lives! "If one does not count the harvest while plowing," reads the Chinese *I Ching,* "nor reflect on the use of the ground while clearing it, then it furthers one to undertake something."

Prayer is one area of life in which the process is all and

the product nothing at all. We don't know anything about the product. That is up to grace. Our call is to get on with the process. We hear the call when we are helpless. Grace is what moves us to admit that we are.

PRAYER

Help me open my heart to you. Amen.

HOW TO PRAY
CONSTANTLY

Be constant in prayer.

ROMANS 12:12

The rhythm of Jesus' life went from action to prayer, from preaching to prayer, from he from confrontation to prayer. Prayer was so vital to life in Christ that Paul urged the Christians in Rome to "be constant in prayer." Grace would enable them to be.

Prayer was one secret of Jesus' creativity. There are two theories about creativity. One says I am the source of my creativity. The other says I am the channel of God's creativity. One says I create. The other says I am used to create. One says creativity is done by me. The other says creativity is done through me.

There is only one argument for taking the channel theory over the source theory. It is the argument that we can be more creative as a channel than as a source. "Dear Lord," Michelangelo prayed as he began painting, "free me of myself, so I can please you."

Prayer makes us more able to cope, more able to live, love, laugh, and be happy. One way we know that is by seeing it in someone else. We see someone whose life is changed by constancy in prayer. We see someone who loves more than we do, laughs more than we do, is happier than we are, is more fully alive.

Prayer went all the way back in Jesus' tradition. The ancient Jews prayed about everything. They held nothing back. They used words for "pray" like cry, sigh, groan, roar, weep, call, praise, boast, sing, exult, rejoice, make merry, hallelujah.

At their most human, the ancient Jews were at their most channeled: they were more creative as channels than they could ever have been as sources. Proof is that, to this day, we worship their God, the infinitely creative one and, arguably, the most creative "idea" in history.

But that God will be elusive if we don't find ourselves in the rhythm of prayer. Jesus had prayed for forty days in the wilderness over whether to be a channel or a source.

Then he no sooner comes out to a life of action than he draws apart "to a lonely place, and there he prayed" (Mark 1:35).

It is in our aloneness that we find ourselves struggling with the question, "Am I a channel or a source?" As grace keeps us constant in prayer, the answer will come.

PRAYER

Help me be constant in prayer. Amen.

HOW TO REPENT

Repent.

MARK 1:15

"Repent," Jesus said in his first sermon in the earliest Gospel. "Repent," he said in his first sermon in Matthew (Matt. 4:17). "Repent," Peter said in the first sermon after Jesus' death (Acts 2:38).

Repentance is turning back. It is what the word meant in the ancient Hebrew. It meant to turn back from injustice, idols, separation from God. We go very far out, and then we turn back. Sin is distance. It is being far from God, from others, even from ourselves. Turn back, Christ says.

242

Come home to yourself. Be the person you were meant to
be. Be fully alive.

But what if we don't feel distant? "I don't see how I
can be a Christian," a young mother said, "because I hon-
estly can't think of any great sin for which I have to repent." Maybe her distance isn't great, but it is still
distance. It manifests itself in anxiety, impatience, irritabil-
ity. These are all telltale signs of being distant from self,
others, God.

Or our distance may show up in being far from what
we want. We may want something so much we cannot live
without it. It may just be life itself. We want to experience
as much of life as possible before we die. We want to be
fully alive. We will do anything to "burst the wild joys of
living against our palate fine," as John Keats wrote.

But will we ever yearn enough? Will we ever hurt
enough—to turn back on our own? "A new heart I will
give you," God says through Ezekiel, "and a new spirit
I will put within you" (Ezek. 36:26). "Return to me,"
God says through Isaiah, "for I have redeemed you"
(Isa. 44:22). "All this is from God," Paul writes of our new
being in Christ (2 Cor. 5:18).

Whenever we repent, it is grace moving us to repent.
Since we will always be too distant from self, others, and
God to be self-motivated to turn back, the power to turn
back has to be God-given. It was the love of the father that
drew the prodigal son home. We don't repent; we find

ourselves repenting. When we find ourselves repenting, it is grace.

PRAYER

When I find myself repenting, help me remember that it is you bringing me home. Amen.

HOW TO DO THE
IMPOSSIBLE

With God all things are possible.

MATTHEW 19:26

B ut how is it possible to believe that? You mean I can
quit my addiction? I can beat my guilt? I can forgive
my boss?

Yes, that is what Jesus is saying. Perhaps it helps to remember where he said it. A rich young ruler has just
turned down Jesus' challenge to sell what he had and give
to the poor. It causes the disciples to wonder, "Who then
can be saved?" (Matt. 19:25). Jesus tells them that "With

God all things are possible"—even for a rich man to sell what he has and give to the poor.

How can we possibly do that? We can't. Only grace can. That was Jesus' point. When it occurs, it has to be grace; it can't be us. It is too big for us. It is even too big for us to sell some of what we have and give to the poor.

Maybe that is the key to Jesus' optimism—seeing grace at work in the little things before we get to the big things. Giving even something to the poor is difficult, particularly if it is substantial enough to affect our lifestyle. We can readily see that we wouldn't be doing it if it weren't grace doing it through us.

This is how grace becomes evident in life. We find ourselves doing things we wouldn't normally be doing. As we see them happening time and again, we begin to see the sense in what Jesus is saying. Then, when the big things come, like addiction, guilt, and anger, we can see how grace can be in them, too.

But how can we tell someone who is dying, "With God all things are possible"? We'd be laughed out of the hospital room. Perhaps. But if the person had seen God all along in the little things, when he or she came to the ultimate big thing, it could be that the words would fit.

The problem with the rich young ruler was that he was young and rich and a ruler. He had not yet had enough experiences of doing the impossible. He could do everything himself. He didn't need grace. Grace was irrelevant.

Eventually, however, if he lived long enough, he would come up against something too big to handle on his own. Then he would need grace. Then grace would move him to discover that "with God all things are possible." We can imagine that he remembered Jesus' challenge and was surprised by grace to find himself selling at least something of what he had and giving to the poor.

PRAYER

Help me remember that all things are possible with you.
Amen.

HOW TO PRAY FOR
SOMEONE

Earnest prayer for him was made ... by the church.

ACTS 12:5

Peter's situation was desperate. He had been arrested, thrown into jail, and chained between two soldiers. The little band of Christians did the only thing they could. "Earnest prayer for him was made ... by the church."

Intercessory prayer is deep within the Judeo-Christian tradition. Abraham intercedes with God on behalf of Sodom and wins (Gen. 18:22-23). Amos intercedes and dissuades God from sending a swarm of locusts (Amos

7:1-3). Moses becomes known as the great intercessor, the one who intercedes with God on behalf of the people (Exod. 32:11-14). The writer of Isaiah 53 incarnates intercession in the Suffering Servant.

In the New Testament, intercession is incarnated in Jesus, who will even intercede on behalf of his executioners, saying, "Father, forgive them" (Luke 23:34). Christians themselves are enjoined to intercede, as they did for Peter. "Confess your sins to one another, and pray for one another," writes the author of James, "that you may be healed" (James 5:16).

But what about praying for someone and it doesn't "work"? One reaction, of course, is to give up on intercessory prayer. Some are healed and some are not, it is argued; and the best we can do is leave the outcome to God. As a matter of fact, we should not be trying to force God's hand with intercessory prayer anyway. What arrogance is it that asks God to break natural law just for us?

Another reaction is to remember that God is so intimately involved with humanity that Jesus could call God "Abba," "Father." Such intimacy implies that God is open to our prayers and that the supernatural can impact the natural at any time. So why be a fatalist? Why not "pray constantly," as Paul advised (1 Thess. 5:17)? Why not try to influence the outcome? Jesus himself said we should pray "importunately," and he used the image of knocking repeatedly on a friend's door at midnight on behalf of another friend (Luke 11:5-6). Our importunity is grace at work.

Miraculously, Peter is freed from prison. "I am sure that the Lord has sent his angel and rescued me," Peter says (Acts 12:11). Did the angel come in response to the earnest prayer made for him by the church? Why not?

PRAYER

Help me pray for others. Amen.

HOW RITUAL WORKS

They found him in the temple.

LUKE 2:46

His parents did not realize that the boy Jesus had stayed behind in Jerusalem at the time of the Passover. When they returned to look for him, "they found him in the temple, sitting among the teachers, listening to them and asking them questions."

We need our rituals, such as going to the temple, to keep us in touch with the transcendent in life and so be fully alive. The word *ritual* has the same root as *harmony, reason, arithmetic.* Things are in harmony when we admit the transcendent. We have a reason for being. Events begin to add up to something.

Worship is one of life's rituals. Once a week we are reminded that things fit together because of grace. Without grace, the disparate strands of life can pull apart.

Prayer is a ritual. A friend of mine had a tough problem. We talked about the ritual of prayer. He was moved to pray as never before. "I prayed not knowing what I was praying for," he said, "but I came out of it with a sense of peace. My only problem," he added with a laugh, "is that I made a lot of promises to God that I don't know how I'll keep!"

Reading the Bible is a ritual. We find ourselves pulling the Bible off the shelf every week, sometimes every day. "There is more in this book that finds me," Lincoln said, "than any other." We are surprised at the insights as various thoughts, feelings, and images make their impact on us.

Alcoholics Anonymous is a ritual. We meet with our small group every week, sometimes twice a week, sometimes every day. It is the power of the small group, discovered by the first-century Christians as *koinonia*. "Bear one another's burdens," Paul wrote, "and so fulfill the law of Christ" (Gal. 6:2).

It is rituals like these that fit the sacred and secular together. When we find ourselves doing them, it is grace, the "higher power" of Alcoholics Anonymous, harmonizing, making life rational, getting things to add up.

PRAYER

Thank you for moving me to perform my daily and weekly rituals. Amen.

HOW TO BEAT
SELF-INTEREST

Where you go I will go.

RUTH 1:16

There are times in life when we want to move beyond self-interest but can't. We're stuck in our own interest.

Ruth's ability to transcend her self-interest is legendary. Instead of returning to her homeland when her husband died, she stayed to console her mother-in-law, Naomi, whose husband had also died. She was able to transcend the claims of her country by moving to another.

And she was even able to transcend the claims of her religion by seeing the value in Naomi's.

The first great controversy in the Christian church was whether Jesus had come for the Jewish nation alone or for all nations. Was the God whom the first Christians worshiped solely a Jewish God or a universal God? "Truly I perceive that God shows no partiality," Peter said (Acts 10:34), whereupon Gentiles received the gift of the Holy Spirit (Acts 10:44).

Ruth defeated her natural tendency to be an egotist, nationalist, and exclusivist. How did she defeat her natural tendency? There can be only one answer. Grace moved her to defeat it. Only grace could move Ruth to say to Naomi: "Where you go I will go, and where you lodge I will lodge; your people shall be my people, and your God my God."

Ruth could not have said that on her own. It was too much to ask of human nature. God's love, however, stops at no individual, national, or religious boundaries. That is what makes it God's love.

The way of love is the way of God. "God is love," the Bible says (1 John 4:16). When we find ourselves loving, it is God in action, grace. When we find ourselves transcending our own self-interest, it is grace doing the transcending through us. So often we ask, "How can I ever experience God?" We are experiencing God when we love, when we find ourselves moving beyond our own self-interest.

So when Jesus said, "I am the way, and the truth, and the life; no one comes to the Father but by me" (John 14:6), what appeared to be the world's most exclusive statement was, in reality, its most inclusive. Jesus was saying that the way of God is the way of unconditional love, which he was incarnating, as had his many-times-great-grandmother, Ruth, before him.

For whom can we be a Ruth?

PRAYER

Thank you for moving me beyond self-interest. Amen.

HOW TO FIND ANSWERS
TO THE BIG QUESTIONS

What do you seek?
JOHN 1:38

When Jesus saw two men following him, he asked them, "What do you seek?" It was an ageless question. What are we looking for—success, money, fame, power, security, happiness, God?

Long before we come to Christ, the big questions come to us. Why are we here? Where are we going? What does it all add up to? It is just such questions that provide the context in which the call of Jesus can be heard. Without such questions, the call may not be heard.

"What do you seek?" It is not only an ageless question but an ultimate one. What concerns us ultimately? Family? Job? Health? Pension? These are all proximate concerns. If we make them ultimate, they become "idols," false ultimate concerns, standing between God and us.

Jesus reminds us that an ultimate concern is about something that will outlast us, specifically, something divine. "Come and see," he tells the two men, indicating the place where he is staying, so they can talk about ultimate things (John 1:39). He wants to attach the men to the next world before they leave this one.

Such an attachment is not meant to disparage this world. "And God saw that it was good," Genesis says repeatedly of this world (Gen. 1:10, 12, 18, 21, 25). Once human beings arrived, it was "very good" (Gen. 1:31). But human beings from the start have tended to stop with this world and not move on to the next.

So when Jesus saw the two men following him, he wanted to get them to see that there was more to life than the mortgage. "What do I seek?" was a question they had been asking all their lives. They had a hunch they could be missing something, which was why they were following Jesus in the first place.

What they were missing was the divine side of their very human lives. They were not yet fully alive. Jesus would give them the divine side. All they had to do was follow him to where he was staying. There they could talk all night.

The night with Jesus was possible because they happened to be standing with John when Jesus happened to walk by. You could call his sudden appearance chance, luck, fate, happenstance, or serendipity. Or, you could call it grace. He has also graced our lives through the happenstance of our birth or of someone telling us about him. Whatever the way, he offers the way—to our divine side.

Martin Luther was in agonizing doubt about his divine side. His confessor told him simply to hold fast to Christ. It worked.

PRAYER

Help me hold fast to Christ with my big questions. Amen.

HOW TO BE A SERVANT

He poured out his soul to death.

ISAIAH 53:12

Isaiah 53 is arguably the most important chapter in the Bible. It is here that the Old and New Testaments come together. Israel as the Suffering Servant becomes, for Christians, Jesus as the Suffering Servant.

With Jesus as our model, Christians are also to be suffering servants. "You will know them by their fruits," Jesus said (Matt. 7:20). We are to feed the hungry, slake the thirsty, welcome the stranger, clothe the naked, and visit the sick and imprisoned (Matt. 25:35-36). Doing so will not only help them but also bring eternal life for us (Matt. 25:46).

By their fruits you shall know them, and the fruits are the fruits of love. Love of God means love of neighbor. "Who is my neighbor?" the lawyer asked Jesus (Luke 10:29). Jesus told him the story of the Good Samaritan, the ideal suffering servant, who cared for an enemy who had been beaten and left at the side of the road.

The first duty of the church, it has been said, is to exist for the world beyond it. Jesus went so far beyond his group of disciples that he ended up on a cross. Churches tend to go less far. They spend, on average, five times more on themselves than on service projects and missions, on going out to those beyond their borders who are hungry, thirsty, strangers, naked, sick, and imprisoned.

Beginning with ourselves as Christians, grace can get us giving a certain amount of time and money to servant-hood. Perhaps it should be a sufficient amount so that we "suffer." The word is in quotes because our suffering will, presumably, be nothing like that of Jesus or the disciples or others who have died for their faith.

Surprisingly, grace never lets Christian servants consider their servanthood to be suffering. "Count it all joy," an early Christian wrote, "when you meet various trials" (James 1:2). Time and again people return from service projects and mission trips saying how much more they received than they gave. Says a friend of mine who leads service trips all over the world, "Service is pure joy."

PRAYER

Help me be a better servant. Amen.

HOW TO HANDLE
LONELINESS

---

*If one member suffers, all suffer together; if one
member is honored, all rejoice together.*

1 CORINTHIANS 12:26

Many people discover they are lonely Christians. They may not belong to a church, or if they do belong, they may not have experienced the deep Christian sharing known as *koinonia*. "If one member suffers," Paul wrote, "all suffer together; if one member is honored, all rejoice together."

A lonely Christian is a contradiction in terms. Christians

262

by definition are members of the beloved community. In that community, people suffer and rejoice together. If we feel lonely, then something is wrong with our relationship to the beloved community.

People feel lonely in churches because they have not been integrated into the life of the church. No one's hurt has become their hurt, no one's laughter their laughter. They don't know anyone at that kind of depth. One reason they don't is that they were left to fend for themselves when they joined the church. They were told to "find their niche," and then they were left to find it.

Most of us need encouragement in the faith. Just as grace moved us to join a church in the first place, so we need grace to bring us a mentor, to do for us what Ananias did for Paul. We need to be invited by some angel to share life in Christ in a small group. *Koinonia* is experienced as people share their lives with one another, their joys and griefs, their guilts and fears. "If one member suffers..." "If one... is honored..."

The reason the first church was so successful is that they had learned how to love in their small groups. All the first churches were small groups. As they shared their new life in Christ, they experienced the love of Christ through one another.

There is a great longing among lonely people for the kind of depth in relationships that comes with sharing the new life in Christ. Such sharing is different from friendship. It is different even from marriage. It is a new kind of relationship, a "new creation," as Paul put it in describing a Christian's relationship to Christ (2 Cor. 5:17).

We can tell we are experiencing the new creation because we feel what Paul called a spiritual glow (Rom. 12:11) and because we find ourselves reaching out to people we never would have reached out to before, healing our own loneliness by reaching out to them in theirs.

PRAYER

Help me find myself reaching out. Amen.

HOW TO PRAY FOR
HEALING

The prayer of faith will save the sick.

JAMES 5:15

It is astonishing, but there it is. "The prayer of faith will save the sick." It is simple, direct, emphatic. We are to pray for the sick and expect results.

The Holy Spirit confers the gift of healing (1 Cor. 12:9). Christ is present through the Spirit. Healing is one form of his presence. Prayer is one form of healing.

We don't fret about whether we have the kind of faith that believes in healing. That's like taking an egg from under a hen, someone has said, and examining it constantly and then wondering why it never hatches.

Our faith is in God, not in our faith. If we can't believe that someone we love will be healed, it does not mean we don't have faith. "It simply means," says Dr. Francis Mac-Nutt, author of the book *Healing,* "that I am willing to admit that I don't know all the factors involved in the situation unless God chooses to reveal them to me." To do otherwise, he says, "is to make oneself into a counterfeit trying to play God."

"Faith," Martin Luther said, "is simply prayer." "Pray for one another," the Bible says, "that you may be healed" (James 5:16). Pray that the infection will leave. Pray that the break will be healed. Pray that the growth of cells needed to restore the diseased part will take place. Grace is moving us to pray specifically.

We do not have to pray with words. We just concentrate on the presence of God in our friend's or loved one's life. We empty the mind and let the love of God flow through us. God will then lead us in what to say and when to say it, if at all.

One thing we will want to do, if grace has brought us to the sick person's bedside, is to affirm God's presence. God is here. Jesus is here. The Holy Spirit is here. And we are here, two or three gathered in Christ's name, being the church, feeling his presence.

"Where two or three are gathered in my name," Jesus said, "there am I in the midst of them" (Matt. 18:20). We are praying in the name of Jesus. It is a powerful prayer. Remember, "The prayer of faith can save the sick."

PRAYER

Help me keep the image of my sick friend joined to the image of Christ. Amen.

HOW TO HANDLE
HEALING THAT DOES
NOT OCCUR

My power is made perfect in weakness.
2 CORINTHIANS 12:9

What if prayer for healing doesn't "work"? What if the patient does not get well? What if the patient dies, as we all will?

Paul had his "thorn in the flesh" about which he "besought the Lord" three times (2 Cor. 12:7-8). He wasn't healed physically, but he was healed spiritually. He heard Jesus say, "My power is made perfect in weakness." His illness kept Paul humble, and it was when he was humble that he was most effective for God.

Maybe we did not pray specifically for what needed to be healed. Maybe we prayed for the wrong thing. Maybe we prayed for someone's healing from addiction to drugs, for instance, when what needed to be healed was the relationship with his or her parents, because the drug use began as teenage acting out.

Maybe our friend or loved one has not been using the normal means of preserving health, and God is saying through the infection that the body needs a rest, that there is a need for more balance in our friend's or loved one's life. Or maybe now is not the time for healing to occur. Or maybe a different person is to be God's instrument of healing. Or maybe we don't know God's timetable. Or maybe God has a different definition of healing.

But God never abandons us. David prayed for the life of his child. It didn't work out, but God never left him. David, as Paul, became a better person, more useful to God. Jesus prayed that he would not have to die. It didn't work out. But God never left him. Indeed, God accomplished something through his death that God could have accomplished no other way.

When healing does not occur, grace can move us to reflect on what God is accomplishing nevertheless. Grace can also move us to keep the faith that healing can still occur. "The medical value of faith is not a matter of faith, but of science," writes Dr. Dale A. Matthews, associate professor of Medicine at Georgetown University School of Medicine and author of *The Faith Factor: Proof of the Healing Power of Prayer*. "More than 300 scientific studies," he writes, "report that religious commitment is associated with better health."

Paul was not healed, but he got something to sustain him in his illness. "My grace," he heard Jesus say, "is all you need" (2 Cor. 12:9 NEB).

PRAYER

May I never lose my faith in your healing power. Amen.

HOW TO HANDLE SIN

They were cut to the heart.

ACTS 2:37

Peter ended the first Christian sermon by accusing the congregation of killing Jesus. "God has made him both Lord and Christ," he told them, "this Jesus whom you crucified" (Acts 2:36). What was their response? "Now when they heard this they were cut to the heart."

All forms of worship include a cut to the heart. Many of them put it toward the beginning of the service. We have to clear the slate with confession of sin before God can write on the slate. The call of Isaiah took place in a worship service. "Woe is me!" we recall his confessing. "For I am lost; for I am a man of unclean lips, and I dwell in the midst of a people of unclean lips" (Isa. 6:5).

What is sin? Sin is separation—from self, others, God, the world around us. The Hebrews carried the definition a step further. They called sin rebellion, willful separation. We willfully separate ourselves from self, others, God, and world. There is something in us compelling us to rebel. That something is what we call sin.

We are reminded of the great public confession of sin by Ezra, in which he recounts the sins of the nation since the time of Abraham. Again and again he reminds the people that they "acted presumptuously" (Neh. 9:29). It was a word that smacked of rebellion.

But he also reminds them with equal vigor that God is "ready to forgive, gracious and merciful, slow to anger and abounding in steadfast love" (Neh. 9:17). The essence of God was that God would forgive sinners. God would overcome the separation. Willfully. It was an astounding act of sheer, unmerited grace.

To underline the point, God made it again, this time not with a nation but with an individual. "Father, forgive them," Jesus says on the cross, "for they know not what they do" (Luke 23:34). He was an incarnation of the divine power to forgive.

When we feel forgiven for our latest rebellion, we are incarnations, too.

PRAYER

May I be conscious of my sin so I can forgive others for their sin. Amen.

HOW TO HANDLE
THE EGO

I am the handmaid of the Lord.

LUKE 1:38

When Mary said she was the handmaid of the Lord, she was using a word the first Christians used to describe themselves. They called themselves "slaves of Christ" (Phil. 1:1, James 1:1, Jude 1:1). The word *hand-maid* was the feminine for *slave*.

The ancient Greeks hated the word *humble*. They would only use it disparagingly. "How can a man be happy," Plato asked in a famous passage, "who is the servant of anything?" There was no place for kneeling in the Greek religion, because it was the attitude of the slave before the master, which was precisely the attitude the early Christians adopted.

The trouble the Greeks had with the Christians' image of the slave was that it took away the ego's power of choice. The number-one virtue for the Greeks was freedom, whereas the number-one virtue for the Christians was obedience. Therefore the perfect image for the first Christians was that of the slave, who had no choice, but whose sole job in life was to do whatever the master, Jesus, ordered.

Needless to say, the Greek and the Christian are still in conflict in us. The queen confronts the handmaid, and we would rather be queen than handmaid. But we grow in life as the queen progressively becomes the handmaid. How does that happen? It happens as we come up against one thing after another that we cannot handle on our own. Only then will we need Jesus.

We cannot save ourselves from the fears that haunt us; we have to be saved. We cannot save ourselves from the perplexities that render us useless; we have to be saved. That is the point of the incarnation, that we are saved, that we can't save ourselves. It's all grace.

The incarnation had to happen in a stable, an image of lowliness. Nothing else would have worked. It had to use a handmaid, an image of humility. Mary didn't will anything. She didn't even participate in her own child's conception. That was how radically the first Christians told the story.

Ironically, it is in our slavery to Christ that we find perfect freedom. As Paul, a slave of Christ, discovered, "For freedom Christ has set us free" (Gal. 5:1).

PRAYER

May I experience the queen becoming the handmaid. Amen.

HOW TO RELEASE THE
INMOST SELF

When Jesus said that "the kingdom of God is within you," he was reminding us that God is not only "out there" but also "in here," not only "wholly other," as some theologians say but also "wholly inner."

The reason the idea of God makes sense in the first place is that it corresponds to something divine in us. Call it the divine spark, call it the image of God, call it what St. Paul did, the "inmost self" (Rom. 7:22), call it the soul—whatever you call it, the kingdom of God is, in Jesus' phrase, "within you."

Consequently, it is of the utmost importance to let what is inside out, to bring to the light of consciousness what is deep within the unconscious. The hidden God of Isaiah needs to be revealed (Isa. 45:15). Jesus' whole ministry was devoted to revealing our inmost depths, to putting us in touch with our souls, to revealing the hidden God.

Our resistance, however, is massive. It may be important to be in touch with our souls, but it seems as though the whole personality is against it. It is perhaps no accident that Jesus uttered his famous statement about the kingdom of God in answer to a question by the Pharisees, the masters of outer as opposed to inner living.

The outer self is the crux of the problem. It competes with the inner for our attention and invariably wins. All we have to do is count the hours we spend each week on the outer life versus the hours we spend on the inner.

The outer life is the life of the ego, the life of jobs and homes and schools and clothes and awards and promotions and raises. All are important, make no mistake. The outer self is not, as some theologians would have it, the "false" self.

There is nothing false about paying the mortgage and putting the bread on the table. The problem is that the outer self so easily usurps the inner, and we lose sight of our souls as we glide through life on the outside, ignoring the depths on the inside.

Focusing on Jesus, who had his outer and inner lives in balance, is one way to recover our souls. How do we do that? Only with help, since we won't do it naturally. How do we know we won't do it naturally? Because we haven't! We've been too busy with the outer life. Our help is grace. When we find ourselves focusing on Jesus, reading passages in the Bible like this one, contemplating them, grace is at work.

PRAYER

Help me focus on Christ. Amen.

HOW TO BECOME A
CHRISTIAN

*When the blood of Stephen thy witness was shed, I
also was standing by and approving.*

ACTS 22:20

Paul could not become a Christian on his own. It was
too much to expect. It wasn't his style. It had to happen to him. He could not make it happen. This was one
thing he could not do. Indeed, he was doing the opposite.
"When the blood of Stephen thy witness was shed," he
told a mob, "I also was standing by and approving."

It took Stephen to show Paul he was on the wrong

track. Stephen showed Paul, suddenly, violently. He was being killed by stoning, while Paul was "keeping the garments of those who killed him." Stephen had dropped into Paul's life, unannounced, to tell him and his friends about Jesus. They had reacted the way many of us do. They became defensive.

Activists need someone who, at great personal risk, will show them they are on the wrong track. They cannot seem to find that out on their own. They are too mesmerized by their myriad activities—from their jobs to their children, their schools, their churches.

Grace appears suddenly in the form of someone who drops, unannounced, into our lives. We could not have predicted such a person. We certainly did not expect such a person. We were simply going about our lives, and the person appeared.

Grace appears, suddenly, in the serendipities of life. These serendipities are objective, beyond us, beyond our ability to cause them to happen. On reflection, we see how they were graceful.

Paul had nothing to do with his conversion. It happened. He did not even let it happen. He was not even open to its happening. "I persecuted the church of God violently," he admitted, "and tried to destroy it" (Gal. 1:13).

The next person who drops, unannounced, into our life could be our Stephen, our messenger from God moving us from antagonist to believer. All we need to do to prepare is—nothing. Just go about our life, as Paul did.

PRAYER

Help me be alert for the arrival of my Stephen. Amen.

HOW TO SACRIFICE

*From everyone to whom much has been given, much
will be required.*

LUKE 12:48 NRSV

Jesus told the parable of a servant to whom the master
had entrusted his possessions while the master was
gone. "From everyone to whom much has been given,"
Jesus said, "much will be required."

The word Jesus used is *required*. Jesus never minced
words. The servant Christian has certain requirements.
One is to give sacrificially. What is sacrificial giving? Giving to the point where it makes a difference in our standard of living.

But we won't do that. We can't meet the requirement. If we come even close, it has to be grace moving us to come close. "If you want to know what grace is," Paul is saying, "find yourself giving until it affects your lifestyle."

Paul got specific as he spoke to the servant Christians of his day about sacrificial giving. He talked about their providing "in abundance for every good work" (2 Cor. 9:8). He talked about their "great generosity" (2 Cor. 9:11). He talked about how sacrificial giving was a test of their faith. "Under the test of this service, you will glorify God by your obedience" (2 Cor. 9:13).

Obedience to requirements is the highest morality for a servant. But it is by no means certain that we will pass the test. Paul knew that giving sacrificially was a test of the affluent Corinthians' spiritual progress. He knew that if they could meet that test they could meet others. If they were obedient now in the requirement of money, they would be obedient later in the requirement of death.

He also wanted them to give because they had been given to. He knew that giving springs from thanksgiving. "Thanks be to God," he writes, "for his inexpressible gift!" (2 Cor. 9:15). He was referring to Jesus.

When we find ourselves giving sacrificially, a spiritual law begins to operate. The more we give, the more we find we have to give. The widow fed Elijah when she didn't have enough, and she had more. The disciples fed the five thousand when they didn't have enough, and there was more than enough. The more you sow, the more you reap. "The one who sows bountifully," Paul writes, "will also reap bountifully" (2 Cor. 9:6 NRSV).

I have never known people who gave sacrificially who didn't say they received more than they gave. One thing they received was dramatic evidence of grace.

PRAYER

Help me give sacrificially. Amen.

HOW TO BE STILL

Be still, and know that I am God.

PSALM 46:10

The word for "be still" in the Hebrew means "to relax." We find a place at home or at work or on our lunch hour and let every muscle in our body untense. "Let go—let God" is a religious cliché, and, like most clichés, it is a cliché because it works for a lot of people.

The word for "be still" in the Hebrew also means "to sink." That gives us an ideal image for relaxing. We talk about being "all geared up" for work. We can gear down as well. Still thinking is deep thinking.

We "scale the heights" all day, trying to "rise to the

top" at our jobs. We try to keep ourselves in "top shape." Why not go to the bottom as well? That's also where the action is. The action is in the inaction.

The cults and Eastern religions are making dramatic advances, particularly among young people. Many have realized that the Judeo-Christian tradition in our culture has largely neglected the idea of being still. When we know by being still, we are meditating. We know by a different way of knowing, not the usual fast-paced way at work and home.

"Be still and know" is not something that comes naturally. We have to be moved to do it. The mover is grace. When we find ourselves being still and "centering down," as the Quakers call it, it is grace moving us to center down.

Brother Lawrence wrote a book in the sixteenth century that is still making the rounds. It is called *The Practice of the Presence of God.* He could be still and know even as he did the dishes. That was how much he had made being still a habit.

Every morning for fifteen years, a friend and his wife have each drawn to a special place in the home where they can be still. They sink into a profound stillness for twenty to thirty minutes, and during that time they sense God arriving.

It boggles our minds to think that God could be as near as our easy chairs.

PRAYER

Help me be still. Amen.

HOW TO HANDLE
SUCCESS

Shall the ax vaunt itself over him who hews with it?
ISAIAH 10:15

The more successful we are, the more necessary God is. When we are successful, we tend to lose sight of God. It is the bootstrap fallacy at work. I did it. I achieved it. I made myself a success. But, Isaiah asks, "Shall the ax vaunt itself over him who hews with it?" Shall we vaunt ourselves over God?

Isaiah saw that God would use Assyria to chasten Israel. The Israelites were enjoying immense prosperity and as a result were losing sight of God. But it was God who had given them the ability to prosper in the first place, and the land in which to prosper in the second place.

St. Augustine put the invisibility of God succinctly in his comments on the demise of Rome. Rome, he said, was felled by "self-love in contempt of God." The ax had vaunted itself over him who hewed with it.

Isaiah saw a "remnant" as the only answer to self-love in contempt of God. The remnant would be charged by grace with responsibility for keeping the faith. Only the remnant could do it. It wasn't for everyone. It was just too hard, too contrary to human nature. As for the rest, their self-destruction was assured. "Destruction is decreed," Isaiah writes (Isa. 10:22).

Grace empowers the remnant to keep God first and success second. When a football player kneels after a touchdown, it is a sign of giving God the glory for the success. That is not a bad image for us whenever we close a deal, get promoted, or praise a child for bringing home good grades.

The letters "AMDG" were often chiseled onto churches. They were the initials of the phrase *Ad Majorem Dei Gloriam,* "To the Greater Glory of God." They meant that the achievement of the builders was not the point. The point was God who gave the builders the ability to build. One could do worse than inscribe those letters over every achievement.

With grace enabling us, the ax will no longer vaunt itself.

PRAYER

Thank you for whatever success I achieve. Amen.

HOW TO HANDLE
SUFFERING

I will show him how much he must suffer.

ACTS 9:16

When suffering happens, so does the question about God. If there is no God, there is no problem. Suffering is simply part of living, and death is part of life. But the more we believe, the more we have a problem. We want an answer to suffering.

One answer is that God set up the kind of world in which suffering *could* happen. God chose to permit it. The alternative was to eliminate free will and natural law, both of which cause suffering. Better to be free and suffer than not to be free and not suffer.

Another answer is to remind ourselves that God set up the kind of world in which suffering *would* happen. It was not only possible but also inevitable. "Human beings are born to trouble," says Job's friend, "just as sparks fly upward" (Job 5:7 NRSV).

A third answer to the problem of suffering is that God set up the kind of world in which suffering *must* happen. It is not only possible and inevitable but also necessary. It is how the hidden God of Isaiah becomes visible (Isa. 45:15). It is not the only way, but one way, and such an effective one that the central symbol of the Christian faith is one of suffering.

"I will show him how much he must suffer for the sake of my name," Jesus says of Paul. "If any want to become my followers," he tells his disciples, "let them deny themselves and take up their cross and follow me" (Matt. 16:24 NRSV). Only grace could move us to follow. To follow is to suffer.

The cross is the key to a fourth answer to the problem of suffering.

God set up not only the kind of world in which suffering could, would, and must happen but also the kind of world in which God would suffer with the sufferers. God chose to suffer. The mystery of the atonement is that God suffers with us. And that makes all the difference.

PRAYER

Help me see you in my suffering. Amen.

HOW TO MAKE A
DIFFICULT DECISION

*His sweat became like great drops of blood falling
down upon the ground.*

LUKE 22:44

Jesus was "in agony" as he prayed about the most important decision of his life, whether to go ahead with
arrest and death. Luke says that he prayed until "his sweat
became like great drops of blood falling down upon the
ground."

The key to his decision lay in God's making it rather
than his making it. "Father, if thou art willing, remove this

cup from me," he prayed (Luke 22:42). His choice would have been to avoid the suffering. But he had been able to pray through to: "nevertheless, not my will, but thine, be done" (Luke 22:42).

It is this praying through that is the key to God's making the decision rather than our making it. It is "agony" to pass beyond our own planning to being planned, beyond controlling our lives to being controlled, beyond active living to passive living, beyond works to grace.

How do we do it? We don't. It has to be done through us, not by us. When we find ourselves praying through, that is grace. It is grace moving us toward the decision through our agony. Our sweat is grace. We often wonder what grace is. This is what grace is. Grace is sweat.

Of course, such a position is at odds with Emersonian self-reliance. Most of us want to say we made the decision ourselves. Emerson's successors, the self-help writers, whisper to us that we can do it. We can eat the apple of self-fulfillment. We can decide.

From the Christian perspective, there is a way to move from decisions made by us to decisions made through us. Someone has to be Jesus for us. Someone has to "die" that we might live. Not in the literal sense, hopefully, but in a certain sense.

The power of the Christian message is that one man was willing to agonize and die to show people how grace was coming to them. His act was then duplicated by Stephen, the first Christian martyr. Stephen's murder gave us Paul, we have seen, just as Christ's decision to leave the garden and die gave us the new life of grace.

A black man went up for communion in an all-white church after the Civil War. The congregation held back. One man who joined his fellow man at the rail. His name? Robert E. Lee.

PRAYER

Help me pray through to you. Amen.

HOW TO HANDLE
TRAGEDY

We were so utterly, unbearably crushed.

2 CORINTHIANS 1:8

What do we do when a friend is struck down with a fatal disease, a loved one dies in a car crash, someone we know is shot in a theft?

Is not the Christian the kind of person who finds God where God is not usually found? Remarkably, tragedy can move us closer to Christ, as Paul discovered. He was "utterly, unbearably crushed," he said; but grace had enabled him to see his suffering as sharing Jesus' own suffering, an insight that brought him the comfort he needed. "As we share abundantly in Christ's suffering," he wrote, "so through Christ we share abundantly in comfort too" (2 Cor. 1:5).

But why should a person want to be closer to Christ? Because grace has shown us how Jesus transformed tragedy. Now grace can show us how to transform our tragedy—by becoming a witness to Christ. "We are afflicted in every way," Paul wrote, "but not crushed; perplexed, but not driven to despair; persecuted, but not forsaken; struck down, but not destroyed; always carrying in the body the death of Jesus, so that the life of Jesus may also be manifested in our bodies" (2 Cor. 4:8-10).

Tragedy can also move us closer to other people, Paul discovered, someone who had spent much of his life killing the very people whom he now loved. "If we are afflicted," he wrote, "it is for your comfort and salvation" (2 Cor. 1:6). "If one member suffers, all suffer together" (1 Cor. 12:26). "Bear one another's burdens, and so fulfill the law of Christ" (Gal. 6:2).

The church is not a group of people who have all the answers when somebody suffers. But it is a group of people who will suffer with the person who is suffering. Christians are the kind of people who will go into the silence where no word comes and into the despair where no hope is and wait with the sufferer for the word and the hope. It was this kind of bearing one another's burdens that so astonished the first church's contemporaries. "Look how they love one another!" a contemporary wrote.

When tragedy strikes, we, too, may be surprised by

grace to discover how much closer we become to other people and to Christ.

PRAYER

Help me keep close to Christ and others when tragedy hits.
Amen.

HOW TO TURN TRAGEDY
INTO VICTORY

*It is not the will of my Father... that one of these little
ones should perish.*

MATTHEW 18:14

When tragedy strikes, we want answers, but they
often come slowly.

If ever we needed grace, now is the time. Eventually,
one answer grace may bring is that God did not do it. God
did not kill our loved one. We cannot blame God. It is not
God's fault.

Nor did God will it. "It is not the will of my Father,"

Jesus said, "that one of these little ones should perish."
"He does not willingly afflict or grieve anyone" (Lam.
3:33 NRSV).

Nor is it fair to blame God for not preventing our
tragedy. This is an argument used against God's existence.
If there were a God, the argument goes, God would have
stopped the cancer. If there were a God, God would have
prevented the plane crash.

But God cannot be drawn to our specifications. Nor
can God repeal the laws of gravity and aging.

The problem when tragedy strikes is that God is inscrutable. "Why dost thou hide thy face?" we cry with the
psalmist (Ps. 44:24). We are dealing with a hidden God,
and we desperately want God to come out of hiding.

Consequently, we turn against God because God, we
feel, has turned against us. "Thou hast cast us off and
abased us...Thou hast made us like sheep for slaughter,
and hast scattered us among the nations" (Ps. 44:9, 11).

God does not will tragedy. But God does allow it. God
set up the kind of world in which tragedy could occur.
God doesn't want it to happen, but God is willing to run
the risk that it can happen. God did not kill Jesus, but God
did allow Jesus to be killed.

God does not will tragedy. God does allow it. And
God is in it. This last is grace's biggest revelation. God was
involved in the death of Jesus, transforming it from
tragedy to victory, from death to resurrection. Similarly,

God is involved in our tragedies, turning them into victories, even though more grace may be needed for us to see them as such.

An American couple's daughter was killed while helping the poor in South Africa. Remarkably, the couple supported the Truth and Reconciliation Commission's grant of amnesty to the four killers, saying they hoped the young men would "receive the support necessary to live productive lives in a non-violent atmosphere." Their ability to plead for amnesty could only have been grace at work in the tragedy, turning it into victory.

PRAYER

Help me see how tragedy can be turned into victory. Amen.

HOW TO HANDLE
TROUBLE

*God is our refuge and strength, a very present help in
trouble.*

PSALM 46:1

One way to handle trouble is to wait. "They who wait
for the LORD," Isaiah said, "shall renew their
strength" (Isa. 40:31). Why wait? Because God will be our
"very present help" in our trouble.

Waiting stimulates the imagination. There are at least
two ways of thinking: the rational and the imaginative.
The one may be called active, the other passive. In the first

we are the subject of our thinking, and in the other we are the object of God's thinking.

Because we spend so much of our lives doing the first kind of thinking, we chafe at the restraints of waiting out the second. Our first thought when we are troubled is, Let's get on with solving our problem. But the wisdom of the ages seems to suggest that, when we are troubled, as the psalmist was, we also would do well to wait so God can arrive.

Remarkably, grace is working on the very images that are troubling us. It is enabling us to wait our images out. If we jump too quickly into troubleshooting, the images won't be able to do their job, which is to get us in touch with the unconscious part of ourselves that we wouldn't be getting in touch with if we were not being troubled. Waiting, then, while intensely imaginative, is also the most "rational" thing we can be doing when we are troubled.

Of course, no one likes to wait. That's why, when we do wait, when we find ourselves waiting, we say it is grace, not us. The psalmist was writing about fear and war, trouble enough for anyone. But he was finding God in the fear and the war, precisely because grace was enabling him to wait long enough for his images to work.

Isaiah was writing around 550 B.C., one of the worst times in Israel's history. Israel had been overrun, and many of its people marched six hundred miles east to Babylonia, where they languished in exile. But God eventually arrived for Isaiah, and the brilliant images of Isaiah chapter 40 are the proof.

Were Isaiah and the psalmist exceptional? Or are they simply living proof that waiting for God in times of trouble can work for any of us?

PRAYER

Help me wait for you in times of trouble. Amen.

HOW TO KEEP THE
MOMENT

Let us make three booths.

MARK 9:5

There are so many moments in life that we want to keep, but they disappear.

The last child goes to kindergarten, and it is quiet in the house. The last child goes to college, and it is quiet again. All our jokes about "a little peace and quiet for a change" cannot cover our loneliness. We go up to our child's room and quietly weep for what cannot be kept.

Jesus and three disciples climbed a mountain, and

there on the mountain, the Bible says, "[Jesus'] garments became glistening, intensely white, as no fuller on earth could bleach them" (Mark 9:3). It was such a significant moment that Peter's reaction was to keep it. "Let us make three booths," he says, in a vain attempt to keep the lasting in the fleeting.

How can we hold those moments in life when the other person is transfigured before us? How can I keep you from growing up? How can I keep you in the same city, the same state? How can I keep you from dying? We will do anything to keep the moment. And everything we do is good. But it goes only so far.

We will build buildings. We will write symphonies and poems and speeches and books. We will go to class re-unions and celebrate anniversaries and birthdays. We will put up stones in graveyards and keep our children's art-work in boxes. We will put photos on walls and write feverishly in journals.

But none of it works. None of it, finally, can keep the lasting in the fleeting. The only way to keep the moment is for grace to give us the faith that it is being kept by God. The moment is eternal because God is. Jesus knew that, so he was unconcerned about making booths. The moment had already been kept. Forever.

How do we get that kind of faith? We don't. It gets us. Only grace can bring it. In the depth of our despair over keeping the lasting in the fleeting, we find ourselves with the faith that the only way the moment can be kept is for God to keep it. God, we sense, is the only permanence in an impermanent world. Our longing to keep the moment is our longing for God. It could be the first time we believed.

PRAYER

Help me see you in each transfiguring moment. Amen.

HOW TO LOVE
UNCONDITIONALLY

His father... ran and embraced him and kissed him.

LUKE 15:20

Unconditional love may be the greatest force in the world, but we say that it is beyond us, that we can't love that way, that only God can. And we are right. When we find ourselves loving unconditionally, it has to be God; it can't be us, because we won't love that way.

Everyone wonders where God is. God is right in our own homes. When our hand is stayed in anger against our child, that's God. It's not us. The prodigal son had no idea what his father would do when he came home after throwing his life away. He knew he had failed. He knew he had not lived up to his father's expectations. But none of that mattered. All that mattered was that he had an image of his father and of going home. "I will arise and go to my father," he said to himself (Luke 15:18).

Something must have gone on in the prodigal son's home to give him that image. He must have experienced unconditional love. That did not mean there might not be punishment. Indeed, he expected it. "Treat me as one of your hired servants," he would say to his father (Luke 15:19).

There is certainly room for judgment in life, but judgment can often be meted out on the inside without having to be inflicted again from the outside. The prodigal son's father knew that. The very sight of his son returning showed him that the boy was coming home to face the music but that he didn't have to play the music because the boy had already heard it.

How could the father know that? Because he was intuitive. How could he have been so intuitive? Because he knew how to love unconditionally. It was dramatic evidence of grace.

When we know how to love unconditionally, we are in tune with our children. We know what they're thinking and feeling. For the boy trudging up the walk, hanging his head, his father knew that he had already judged himself, so he didn't need to do any more judging.

What he did need to do was show his son that he loved him for who he was in spite of what he did—that he loved him "prodigally."

He does something fathers in our culture are not noted for doing. He shows his son his feelings. "While he was yet at a distance," Jesus says, "his father saw him and had compassion, and ran and embraced him and kissed him."

PRAYER

Help me love unconditionally. Amen.

HOW TO GO DEEP

Where do you get that living water?

JOHN 4:11

On the mountains of Colorado, high on the tundra, you can find an exquisite flower, the spring beauty. It is only half an inch high, but its root is three feet. The only way the spring beauty survives is to have its root go deep, to where the water is. There would be no beauty if there were no root.

We are intrigued by the depths of who we are because we have a hunch that, like the root of the spring beauty, it is our depths that define us. We feel there is a plan for our lives, and our task in life is to find it and act on it. We have this feeling, as Shakespeare put it, that "there is a destiny that shapes our ends, rough hew them how we will." "Before you were born," God tells Jeremiah, "I consecrated you" (Jer. 1:5).

Psychosis is what can happen when we do not take the depths of who we are seriously and when those depths erupt. There is also world psychosis, which is constantly erupting. Fifty million people were killed in World War II. Ten million in World War I. Still others in Vietnam, Iraq, Bosnia, Afghanistan, Egypt, Syria. If we do not take the depths of who we are seriously, then we are in grave danger of withering at our roots.

It took God in the form of Jesus to show the woman at the well who she really was, to reveal her hidden depths to herself, to get her in touch with that "living water" that could nourish her roots for the rest of her life. She wanted to argue with him about theology, but he gently led her into her depths, revealing her inner beauty to herself.

Grace can lead us into our hidden depths too, as we find ourselves reading stories in the Bible like this one and as we find ourselves being led to someone more mature in the faith who can reveal the living water to us. It is quite possible that such a person will come into our lives serendipitously, as Jesus did, in his chance encounter with the woman at the well. Coincidence, it has been said, is God acting anonymously. It is also God acting gracefully.

PRAYER

Help me encounter the depths of who I am. Amen.

HOW TO BE A CHURCH

These people... have been turning the world upside down.

ACTS 17:6 NRSV

Jesus' Great Commission to the church was to "make disciples of all nations" (Matt. 28:19). One way the first church made disciples was by finding themselves following a three-fold discipline motivated by grace. They were so successful at it that a mob in Greece said they were "turning the world upside down."

For one thing, the first church studied. "They devoted themselves to the apostles' teaching" (Acts 2:42). A disciple is a learner in the root sense of the word. The Christian church begins and ends with the Bible, but we can't understand the Bible unless we study it, just as we can't understand our jobs unless we study them.

The first church also shared. "They devoted themselves to the apostles' teaching and fellowship." "If one member suffers," Paul wrote, "all suffer together. If one member is honored, all rejoice together" (1 Cor. 12:26). "Bear one another's burdens," he said, "and so fulfill the law of Christ" (Gal. 6:2).

All the first churches were small groups. All experienced the deep Christian fellowship known as *koinonia* right in their own homes. Only when your hurt becomes my hurt, only when my grief becomes your grief, only when your tears and your laughter become my tears and my laughter, only then will we experience *agape*, the Christian love for which the first church became famous.

The first church also served. "I am among you," Jesus sad, "as one who serves" (Luke 22:27). "Whoever serves me, the Father will honor" (John 12:26 NRSV). Jesus himself was called the Suffering Servant, and every church member is called to servanthood in Christ's name, taking on something in social service and social action to feed the hungry, clothe the naked, heal the sick, and welcome the stranger (Matt. 25:35).

"What the world expects of Christians," wrote atheist philosopher Albert Camus, "is that [they] should speak out loud and clear,... in such a way that never a doubt, never the slightest doubt, could rise in the heart of the simplest [person]. . . . They should get away from abstraction and confront the blood-stained face history has taken on today."

As the current church finds itself as disciplined by grace as the first church, many more disciples will be made.

PRAYER

Help me study, share, and serve Christ. Amen.

HOW TO WITNESS

Come and see.

It's right there at the beginning of the Gospel of John, one of the most compelling stories in the Bible about how to be a witness. Jesus finds Philip. Philip finds Nathaniel. Then Philip brings Nathaniel to Jesus.

All it takes to be a witness is to be found by Jesus. Jesus "found Philip," John records, "and said to him, 'Follow me'" (John 1:43). How Philip would follow would be to share the good news of what had happened. "We have

316

found him of whom Moses...and...the prophets wrote," he exclaims to Nathaniel (John 1:45).

Ironically, Nathanael rejects Philip. "Can anything good come out of Nazareth?" Nathaniel sneers. It was inconceivable that anything so stupendous as the Messiah could come out of a rival town eight miles north.

But grace has Philip persist. He utters the classic invitation of the witness: "Come and see." Come to church with me. Come and meet the one who introduced me to Christ. Come to my small group that meets every month to pray and read the Bible and talk about Jesus.

Here is where we falter. Too often we take our rejection for an answer. But Philip not only persists but also resists the temptation to argue. All he does is issue the invitation: "Come and see." He knows that whether Nathaniel comes is up to grace. He does not need to do more.

Nathanael does come. We assume he was Philip's friend and that if something was that important in Philip's life, it might also be in his. That was why he came.

Ten thousand people were asked why they became church members. One percent said they had been to a crusade; another 1 percent said they had been visited by a church member. Two percent said they had a special need that brought them. Three percent said they just walked in; another 3 percent said they liked the church's program. Five per cent said they liked the Sunday school; 6 percent said they liked the pastor. But a whopping 79 percent said they joined the church because a relative or friend brought them.

To be sure, witnessing is never easy and the results never sure. But let's not prejudge the outcome. All we have to do is issue the invitation. "Come and see." Grace will do the rest. As Jesus promised Nathanael, "You will see heaven opened" (John 1:51). It doesn't get much better than that.

PRAYER

May I have the courage to witness and leave the outcome to you. Amen.

HOW TO WITNESS
TOGETHER

*There were added that day about three thousand
souls.*

ACTS 2:41

When we find ourselves witnessing, it is grace using
the Holy Spirit. How do we know? Because we
wouldn't be witnessing on our own. The first Christians
found themselves witnessing only when the Holy Spirit arrived at Pentecost. Then they were so effective that "there
were added that day about three thousand souls."

How can we be that effective? By finding ourselves

paying attention to how the first Christians became effective. First, they were waiting for the Holy Spirit. Jesus had told them to do nothing but wait (Acts 1:4). That is how the Holy Spirit would come.

Second, they were all together. One hundred and twenty of them were in the upper room. There was something about waiting together that inspired them. Our ability to witness effectively comes from waiting with others for the gift of the Holy Spirit.

Third, they prayed as a group. Most of us don't. We are missing a powerful experience. It was their praying together that was a gift of the Holy Spirit. Once inspired, they were then able to witness effectively.

One of them was particularly effective. Peter found himself telling about Jesus. He was so effective that the crowd "were cut to the heart" (Acts 2:37). Their emotion inspired them to ask, "What shall we do?" "Repent," Peter found himself saying, "and be baptized" (Acts 2:38).

To be effective, our witness needs to stir others' emotions. It must inspire them to act upon what they have heard. Naturally, we don't think we can possibly be that effective. But that is not the point. The point is to find ourselves praying with other people while we wait for the Spirit. That is all that is needed to become effective.

But we don't believe it. We feel there has to be more. It can't be that simple. Just wait with other people and pray? Yes, that's how it all began. It's how the first

Christians became effective witnesses for Christ. It's how we can become effective, too.

I belonged to a group of twenty or so who would wait every Sunday night. We would share our experiences with Christ in the previous week. Then we would pray. It was powerful. One night we met in a home in a run-down area of the city. We had bought the home. Then we bought another. Then another. Then we bought a hotel. We opened its doors to the poor. Eventually, several city blocks were a witness to what the Spirit could do through a group of Christians who had waited together and prayed.

PRAYER

May I find myself waiting and praying with others. Amen.

HOW TO DO GOOD WORKS

Let your light shine before others, so that they may see
your good works
MATTHEW 5:16 NRSV

Good works are, in a sense, passive acts. "The Son can do nothing," Jesus said, "of his own accord" (John 5:19). These passive acts are the powerful ones.

In Isaiah 53 and the Gospels, good works are done *through* the servant figure rather than *by* him. As a later servant, Paul, was to say: "I will not venture to speak of anything except what Christ has wrought through me" (Rom. 15:18).

Christians are called to be servants. We are called to do good works. "Let your light shine before others," Jesus

said, "so that they may see your good works." He did not
say, "so that they may see your faith."

Paul expanded on the works idea. God "will render...according to [each one's] works," he wrote (Rom.
2:6). He did not say "according to each one's faith." "If I
have all faith...but have not love, I am nothing" (1 Cor.
13:2). Christians would prove their faith through love.

But who ever loves enough? No one. That is why we
cannot be saved by works, only by grace. Grace moves us
to works, just as it moves us to faith. But the faith is faith-
less without the works. The work validates the faith.
"Faith apart from works," an early Christian wrote, "is
dead" (James 2:26).

Even though we cannot love enough, it is remarkable
what grace can do through us. Jesus amazed his disciples
by saying, "Very truly, I tell you, the one who believes in
me will also do the works that I do and, in fact, will do
greater works than these" (John 14:12 NRSV).

What could he have had in mind? We have no way of
telling. But we do know that his faith in grace was such
that he could say, "If you have faith as a grain of mustard
seed, you will say to this mountain, 'Move hence to yon-
der place,' and it will move; and nothing will be impossible to you" (Matt. 17:20). Talk about works! Grace is
moving us to move mountains.

PRAYER

May I find myself moving a mountain. Amen.

HOW TO SUCCEED IN FAITH

This is not your own doing.

EPHESIANS 2:8

No matter how hard we work, we are not going to make it in the religious dimension. We are not going to turn the other cheek. We are not going to go the second mile. We are not going to sell what we have and give to the poor.

These are impossible expectations. That does not mean they are not valuable. It only means they are not possible. Indeed, their value lies in their impossibility. "With [people] it is impossible," Jesus said, immediately after telling the rich man to sell what he had and give to the poor (Mark 10:27). "But not with God," he added, "for all things are possible with God." That was the point.

Yes, works are important. Giving to the poor is important. But we never give enough. The point of the works is to show they don't work. We can't do them. We can't measure up. The point is to show us the limits of the active and throw us onto the passive.

When even approximations of obeying Jesus occur, they can't be us; they have to be grace. Grace is doing the work through us. "This is not your own doing," the Bible says regarding faith, "it is the gift of God." Faith could not be a work any more than obedience. Each was a gift. "By grace you have been saved through faith."

We succeed in faith when we are less the actor and more the acted upon, when we are less the potter and more the clay, less active and more passive. We succeed when we are "born again," a totally passive action (John 3:3). We can't bring about our own births, and we can't bring about our own faith or works. It is all grace, all gift.

Succeeding in faith is a matter not of the Pharisee who says, "I can," but of the disciple who says, "I can't." It is a matter not of the active person, who says, "I do," but of the passive person, who says, "It can only be done through me." "This is not my own doing," the passive person says. "I worked harder than any of them," Paul explains, "though it was not I, but the grace of God which is with me" (1 Cor. 15:10).

All credit to God; no credit to Paul. That is how we succeed in faith.

PRAYER

Help me see grace in my faith and works. Amen.

HOW TO BE WHOLE

The Son of man came to seek and to save the lost.

LUKE 19:10

Part of us is lost to us. It is the part that can only be found through religion. The word *religion* comes from the root for "bind back." Through our religion we are bound back to the lost part of who we are, the passive part, the part we don't control but that controls us, the part through which God comes into view.

It was no accident that Jesus chose the sheep as his controlling metaphor. Nor that God chose a baby for incarnation. Nor that the first Christians referred to

327

themselves as "slaves." Sheep implied shepherd. Baby implied parent. Slave implied master.

The sheep was incomplete without the shepherd, the baby without the parent, the slave without the master. What God did, through Jesus, was save us from incomplete living by moving us, in the events of our everyday lives, from active to passive living, from the part of ourselves we knew about to the lost part of ourselves we didn't know about. God makes that movement through grace, God in action.

Zaccheus is a case in point. He was a "chief tax collector" (Luke 19:2). Tax collectors could charge whatever they wanted. Because they extorted, they were despised and not allowed in the synagogues. But the chance event of Jesus' arrival in town shot Zaccheus up a tree to see him.

When Jesus saw Zaccheus, Jesus told him that he would stay at his house. Over dinner, Zaccheus said he would return everything he had stolen, and he'd return it "fourfold" (Luke 19:8). Jesus had restored the lost part of who he was to Zaccheus. The chance event of Jesus happening into town was pure grace. For the first time, Zaccheus was fully alive.

Earlier, Jesus had likened a lost sheep to "one sinner who repents" (Luke 15:7). The word *repent* in Hebrew means to "turn." When we "don't know where to turn," it is possible we are being turned. When that happens, the recovery of a lost part of who we are can happen, as it did for the repentant Zaccheus, one whom Jesus called "lost."

Repentance is not something we can do on our own. If we could, we would have done it long ago. The active person feels no need to repent. Everything is under control. But when our passive side is recovered by grace, when the shepherd finds the sheep, then the passive side of who we are unites with the active, the lost is found, and, at least for the moment, we are whole. We are fully alive.

Any chance event can be graceful. It can even be a turning point. The arrival of Jesus in town became a turning point for Zaccheus. He found himself repenting. The shepherd had found his lost sheep. Zaccheus had found the lost part of Zaccheus.

We, too, can be found. We, too, can be surprised by grace. We, too, are being sought by grace through the everyday events of our lives.

PRAYER

Help me see your grace in everyday events. Amen.

HOW TO ATONE

My tongue will sing aloud of thy deliverance.

PSALM 51:14

One way to handle our separation from God is to atone for those things we have done to create the separation in the first place. That way we can be "at one" with God again.

The writer of Psalm 51 had an acute sense of sin. "My sin is ever before me," he writes (Ps. 51:3). But he also had an acute sense of the possibility of forgiveness. "Create in me a clean heart, O God, and put a new and right spirit within me" (Ps. 51:10). Forgiveness, however, is worthless without atonement. No "cheap grace," as Bonhoeffer put it.

"I will teach transgressors thy ways," the psalmist says. It was a new way of looking at things. Usually, a lament over sin ended with a thank offering in the presence of the congregation. But that was not enough for this sinner. He would teach other people how not to go wrong as he had. His teaching would be his atoning.

"My tongue will sing aloud of thy deliverance." Teaching was one thing, singing another. The "joy" he felt in "salvation" could not be contained (Ps. 51:12). It would break forth in song, which is why churches sing joyous songs. The worshipers are celebrating the joy of their salvation.

"My mouth shall show forth thy praise" (Ps. 51:15). It was an allusion to leprosy. Restored to the fellowship of the congregation, the cleansed leper would praise God in worship. Now the psalmist, purged, washed, and with a clean heart, can do the same.

But he will not give that thank offering. His sin is too big and any offering too small. Besides, it would be liturgical rather than visceral. What was visceral was a broken spirit. "The sacrifice acceptable to God," he says, "is a broken spirit" (Ps. 51:17). He who had left God was now back with God because the depth of his sorrow had reached the depth of his sin.

What was his motivation to atone? Grace. Remember,

we can't rescue ourselves from our sin. "God's kindness," Paul wrote, "is meant to lead you to repentance" (Rom. 2:4). "It depends not on [human] will or exertion," he explained, "but upon God's mercy" (Rom. 9:16). "A new heart I will give you," God says through Ezekiel, "and a new spirit I will put within you" (Ezek. 36:26). God works through grace to move us to confess, then to repent, and, finally, to atone. Without the atonement, the confession and repentance would not work.

PRAYER

Thank you for moving me to atone. In the name of the one who atoned for me, Amen.

HOW TO GIVE OURSELVES

She has done a beautiful thing to me.
MARK 14:6

Jesus was eating with his friend when a woman came in with an alabaster jar of pure nard. It was the custom at fashionable dinners to anoint the hair, beard, and feet with fragrant oils. This oil was from a rare plant in India. The woman broke the jar and poured the oil over Jesus' head.

She could have used a few drops rather than the whole jar and a cheap perfume rather than a costly one. She gave everything, in other words, when she could have given something. She gave more when she could have given less.

She was lavish when she could have been careful, extravagant when she could have been prudent. It was, Jesus said, "a beautiful thing."

We do not give ourselves as much as we know we should. We hold on to ourselves. We won't let ourselves go. We won't break ourselves open for somebody else. But beauty is in the lavish giving of ourselves to others. Only two other people are praised by Jesus, and both are similar examples of extravagance—the widow who gave all that she had (Mark 12:43) and the centurion who came to him brokenhearted for his dying servant (Matt. 8:10).

Jesus gave himself to people. He broke the jar constantly. His death is the ultimate symbol of the broken jar. "This is my body, which is broken for you" (1 Cor. 11:24 KJV). Christians are to give themselves in what Dietrich Bonhoeffer called "love to the uttermost." He lived out the title of his best-known book, *The Cost of Discipleship,* when he was hanged by the Nazis.

It may be objected, of course, that these are extreme examples. Clearly, we are not expected to give up our lives or all that we have. Maybe not. But the principle is the same—giving ourselves away, from the smallest to the biggest things in life. When we find ourselves doing that, it is graphic evidence of grace. How so? Because we know we wouldn't do it on our own.

The image of the woman breaking the jar can move

us to do the same. Suddenly, one day, we will find ourselves being lavish. It will be pure grace.

PRAYER

May I find myself breaking the jar. Amen.

ABOUT THE AUTHOR

Robert K. Hudnut is a Presbyterian pastor and author living in Cottage Grove, Minnesota, a suburb of St. Paul. He is the author of twelve books on faith and the church. He has served churches in Winnetka, Illinois; Minnetonka, Minnesota; and Albany, New York. He is a summa cum laude graduate and former trustee of Princeton University.